MANUAL
OF
JAPANESE FLOWER ARRANGEMENT

BY
JOSUI OSHIKAWA
AND
HAZEL H. GORHAM

CULTURAL EXCHANGE CLUB
NISHI-GINZA, CHUŌ-KU,
TOKYO, JAPAN.

Copyright, 1936, by NIPPON BUNKA RENMEI
First Printing June 1936.
Copyright, 1951, by CULTURAL EXCHANGE CLUB
Third Printing June 1951.

COPYRIGHT IN JAPAN
PRINTED IN JAPAN

Printed by
THE BENRIDO CO., LTD., KYOTO.

PREFACE

Culture is, so to speak, a bouquet of beautiful flowers dedicated to mankind by Nature, giving comfort and significance to human life. The way of flower arrangement can well be called an elegant and representative art created and fostered for ages by the Japanese. It is regarded not only as a national art among all classes of Japanese but also as a universal way of elevating the mind to spiritual beauty and perfection through the medium of pure and beautiful flowers created by the hand of God.

It is the way of flower arrangement that enables men to grasp Nature in her most beautiful aspect and to purify and beautify their spirits. Flowers are symbolical of the true and creative life of Nature ; the way of flower arrangement is indeed a universal way pervading all Japanese hearts, regardless of class or calling. If the consideration of flowers is excluded, no significant side of real Japanese life can be understood.

Our love for flowers in beautiful arrangement is perhaps due to our time-honoured outlook on life, our feeling that Nature and Culture are inseparably united.

It is a great pleasure for us that Japanese flower arrangement is to be introduced to foreign nations through the collaborated efforts of Mrs. Josui Oshikawa, head of the Sho-fu-ryu school, and Mrs. Hazel H. Gorham. We are well aware how conscientious

v

and painstaking their labours have been. The successful achievement of this difficult work is, we believe, due to their keen insight into Japanese Culture and their love for Nature and Mankind as well.

It is hoped that this Manual may prove a beautiful flower, blooming out of our unique Japanese Culture, and dedicated to the minds and hearts of the world.

GAKU MATSUMOTO,

President of the Nippon Bunka Renmei

Tokyo,
June 17th, 1936

FOREWORD

Flower arrangement is an art and as such belongs to the world. Its enjoyment should not and cannot be confined to any one people. The love of flowers is universal, but it has been left to the Japanese to develop the technique of their arrangement. In Japan this art has been practised for centuries, and books without number have been written about it. The purpose of the present volume is to put before the English-speaking world a simple explanation of the fundamental rules governing the Japanese method of flower arrangement, so that flower lovers everywhere may derive increased pleasure from the flowers of their own land.

It is an axiom that art cannot be confined to rules—yet all great art is based on certain definite principles, within which is infinite variety. So with Japanese flower arrangements; no two are ever alike, though all are based on the self-same principles.

This book will have served its purpose if it succeeds in rousing its readers to a further study of this fascinating art, and in encouraging them to adapt the Japanese method to their own material and spiritual requirements. To this end only basic lessons are given and but few substitutes of plant material suggested. The flower arrangements illustrated were made in Japan, of Japanese materials to suit Japanese requirements, and are intended as suggestions for using plant material available in our readers' own country,—not to be copied blindly. For a Japanese flower arrangement to be true to the teaching of this art, it must first of all express the spirit of its arranger and its surroundings.

FOREWORD

In these days of " wars and rumours of wars " the world is tired of materialism and eager for peaceful achievements. A common interest makes for friendship. Art is international, it has no boundaries. The art of flower arrangement belongs to the world, and the authors of this book will count themselves fortunate if their years of pleasant mutual labour become a prototype for the contact of their respective countries.

JOSUI OSHIKAWA

HAZEL H. GORHAM

Tokyo,
June, 1936

MANUAL

OF

JAPANESE FLOWER ARRANGEMENT

ACCORDING TO

IKE-NO BO AND SHO-FU-RYU

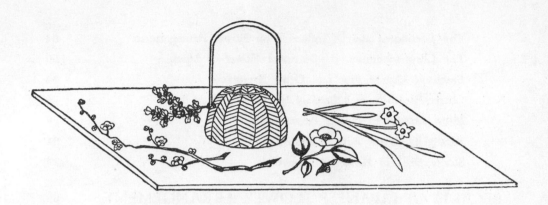

CONTENTS

xi

ILLUSTRATIONS

FLOWER ARRANGEMENT
THROUGHOUT THE AGES

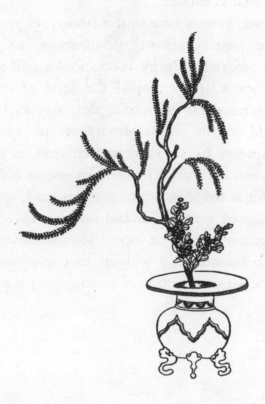

JAPANESE flower arrangement is the result of centuries of development, and the successive stages are not clearly recorded. The facts here set forth are the findings of a painstaking search of old books, for, like the Japanese code of ethics, *Bushido*, which was not even named until the late Inazo Nitobe attempted to explain it to the American President, Theodore Roosevelt, flower arrangement was accepted and no need was felt for explanation. The average Japanese no more questions the meaning of flower arrangement than he does the institution of marriage—it exists, that is enough.

There has never been a time in the history of the Japanese nation when some form of flower arrangement has not been practised. At first enjoyed only by court nobles and priests, by the fourteenth century it had permeated the mass of the people, and to-day even the humblest household will have its formal, set arrangement to add to the festive atmosphere of any holiday. The first thing a Japanese baby's wandering eye rests on is a flower arrangement and when the man has closed his eyes in his last sleep a flower arrangement is the silent sentinel at his head, symbolising by its shape and material eternal life and peace. There is no occasion too trivial, or too solemn, to have a suitable flower arrangement sanctioned by custom, and without this something would be lacking. To the Japanese a flower arrangement is a necessity, not a luxury.

There are many and conflicting records of the origin of the art of flower arrangement. Admittedly an importation, together with so many other forms of art, in the middle of the sixth century, to-day it has no existence outside Japan. Always attributed to Buddhist teachings, there is no trace of it in any of the other so-called Buddhist countries. In Siam can be found a kind of flower arrangement, but totally different from the Japanese in form and feeling ; flowers are ruthlessly sacrificed for an hour's enjoyment and only scent and colour are considered. While it is claimed that flower arrangement originated in China, there is to-day no trace of the art in that country, except a few old books on the subject, and some beautiful flower vases and baskets. The Chinese, like their pupils, the Japanese, have an intense love of all forms of nature, especially blossoms, but they never developed a method of arranging them. The Japanese accepted the idea of flower arrangement from their Chinese neighbour, made it their own, modified, developed and vitalised it in harmony with their racial characteristics.

It is interesting to note that two great religions, Shintoism and Buddhism, contributed to the development of flower arrangement in Japan. The great use of the pine and bamboo and other evergreens in the flower arrangement compositions of to-day undoubtedly traces back to the *Shinto* idea of simplicity and love of nature. Buddhism, on the contrary, delights in gorgeousness and ostentation, and Japanese flower arrangements to-day are the result of these two influences. *Shinto* floral offerings are known as *Shinka* but this method never made any progress ; it continues to use simple evergreen branches ; *Bukka* or the method developed by Buddhist priests is to-day a living influence.

When Buddhism entered Japan, about the middle of the sixth century, it brought with its religious teachings the custom of offering flower petals to the gods. In India flowers are sweet-scented, and perhaps due to climatic reasons, no attempt is made to offer

5

them as living flowers ; they are stripped from their stems and the petals placed in jars or vases. The gods are thought to enjoy the lovely odours. China accepted this custom without protest and passed it on to Japan, but here it came into opposition with the primitive *Shinto* custom of offering small evergreen seedlings, roots and all. Both the *Kojiki* and *Nihon Shoki*, two of the oldest historical records in Japan, make mention of uprooted *sakaki* trees, decorated with the mirror, the jewels and the sword (the Imperial Insignia of to-day), being offered to the gods in the performance of religious services to the spirits of the ancestors.

And another historical book states that on the death of Izanagi-no-mikoto an offering of flowers was made to his departed soul. It is interesting to note that it is stated that flowers were " sacrificed " to the gods, showing the primitive Japanese idea of regarding flowers as living entities. That the idea of preserving the life of the flowers was the influence behind the Japanese flower arrangement is partly proved by the general term applied to all kinds of flower arrangements—*Ike-bana*, the characters for which can be read " Living Flowers." Though developed under the influence of religion, flower arrangement to-day has lost all such associations, and it is now considered a necessary accomplishment of all well-bred people.

Flower-arrangement enthusiasts claim that the very earliest record of the practice of this art in Japan is to be found in the story of Amaterasu-Omikami, the Sun goddess, who gave command to the ancestors of the present Imperial House to rule over the land of Japan for ages eternal. According to this story the Sun goddess, annoyed by the rudeness of her younger brother, Susanoo-no-mikoto, retired into a cave and closed the rock door behind her.

6

This act of hers threw the land of Japan into darkness and the myriads of gods were troubled and consulted together as to the best method of enticing her out again. Then one of the wise gods proposed that they erect a tree before the cave and decorate it with the jewels and the mirror and coloured cloths, and display it before the retreat of the Sun goddess. So amusingly did the dancer goddess entertain the myriad gods that they roared with laughter and the Sun goddess peered forth from her cave in amazement at their apparent disregard of her anger. Lured by the beauty of the tree she took a step forward, when the god of strength deftly barred her return to the cave by closing the entrance with a rope of straw. Thus light was again restored to the world, and the myriads of gods rejoiced.

Historical tradition assigns the date 540 A.D. to the first record of flowers being placed in water for religious offerings, but it is quite likely that the set formal arrangement, forerunner and prototype of to-day's arrangements, was not developed until after the introduction of Buddhism in the middle of the sixth century. Certain it is that from that time onwards flower arrangement was accepted as a form of art necessary for the proper observance of Buddhist ceremonies.

The Japanese readily accepted the Buddhist teaching of the unity of all animate life and added to it the concept of the unity of inanimate life as well. They have a great love of nature in all its manifestations. Although it cannot be said that nature particularly favours Japan, subject as the land is to elemental disturbances, still the Japanese have no fear of its power, and this perhaps explains the hold that flower arrangement has had on the people throughout these many centuries, for a flower arrangement is never merely a setting forth of flowers for the adornment of the house, it is an attempt to bring a bit of nature into the house, a suggestion of nature's grandeur and power.

The oldest known school of flower arrangement in Japan has an authentic history of thirteen centuries. Its founder, Ono-no-Imoko, was a member of the Imperial Court and one of the envoys sent to China to study that country's civilisation. His patron, Shotoku-Taishi, was an ardent Buddhist, and during the reign of his aunt, the Empress Suiko, that religion became firmly entrenched in Japan. It was under the enlightened rule of this great Empress that Japan received many forms of civilisation from China, then at the beginning of the Tsang dynasty and perhaps at the point of its greatest cultural development; literature, drama, painting, sculpture, all the arts, flourished and Japan was China's receptive pupil.

Among the many forms of art received at this time was that of gardening, and this Chinese influence is plainly traceable in the gardens of to-day; but whether the art of flower arrangement came in at that time or is a development truly Japanese, is a doubtful question, and one not likely to be settled immediately. Certain schools of flower arrangement in Japan claim their origin in

China, but it is far more likely that Japanese flower arrangement is the result of an adaptation of Chinese art principles to the Japanese love of nature.

On the death of Shotoku-Taishi, Ono-no-Imoko resolved to devote the rest of his life to praying for the repose of his patron's soul. Shotoku had caused a garden to be made following the Chinese models, with a lake, and Ono-no-Imoko shaved his head and retired to this garden and built for himself a hermitage ; here night and morning he held services before the tablet of his friend and spent his days in meditation.

Now, an indispensable part of a Buddhist service is a floral offering and Ono-no-Imoko conceived the idea that it was not right to offer flowers carelessly to the Buddha ; he taught that care should be taken in their arrangement. It was not sufficient merely to prolong their life, they should be made to express, or symbolise, the part that the love of flowers played in harmonising man and nature, spirit and matter. As he studied and taught, other priests came to copy his floral arrangements, so within his lifetime his method of arranging flowers was widely used, and those who followed his way said that their arrangements were in the style of the offering in the hermitage by the lake, or *Ike-no-bo*, thus giving a name to the first school of flower arrangement. Both name and school are in existence to-day. To understand the persistence of this method one must consider the attitude of the Japanese people towards a teacher, or a master in any line of endeavour ; they have a great respect for ability, and the continuance of an idea or ideal is ensured by their adherence to a master's teachings. It must not be thought that this is an unthinking adherence ; each successive master of the *Ike-no-bo* school made some slight modification in form, while retaining the basic principles, so that the *Ike-no-bo*

9

arrangements of to-day bear but a slight resemblance to those of Ono-no-Imoko's time. But the underlying idea of Japanese flower arrangement, that the nature of the plant material and the individuality of the arranger must be expressed, and that the arrangement must symbolise some philosophical idea, has never been lost sight of ; and a book in the possession of the authors, of drawings of *Ike-no-bo* arrangements, published by the fortieth master at Kyoto, just a century ago, could almost serve as a model for to-day's arrangements. The only alteration necessary would be a slight lengthening of the *Tai* branch.

The history of the growth and development of Japanese flower arrangement can best be understood in conjunction with the spread of Chinese culture in Japan. At the time of its introduction the Imperial Court was composed mostly of the forefathers of the present Imperial family. There has always existed in Japan a peculiar system of delegating authority to persons lower in rank and this was already in operation. The Emperor was the chief patriarch of a group of patriarchal clans each within itself autonomous, with the leader responsible to the Emperor for its members ; and these leaders or clan chiefs (*Uji-no-kami*) looked to the chief patriarch for help and advice. Accustomed to taking the lead in all matters pertaining to the welfare of the Japanese people, when the wave of Chinese civilisation reached these shores in the sixth century the Imperial patriarch delegated to different clan chiefs the development of different arts. This is the earliest recorded manifestation of a peculiar trait of the Japanese people, their dependence on a higher authority for guidance. The Imperial Court of Japan has always taken the lead in introducing new forms of culture to the mass of the people. This is strikingly illustrated by the action of Emperor Meiji when he, riding the crest of the wave of European civilisation in the twentieth century, issued the " Imperial Oath of the Five Principles ":

(1) Public meetings shall be organised, and administrative affairs shall be decided by general deliberation.

(2) Governors and governed alike shall devote themselves to the good of the nation.

(3) All civil or military officials shall endeavour to encourage individual industries in all classes, and to call forth their active characteristics.

(4) Defective customs hitherto prevailing shall be corrected.

(5) Useful knowledge shall be introduced from the outside world and thus the foundation of the empire shall be strengthened and stabilised.

Before public opinion had been formulated this wise leader foresaw the trend of the times and granted the people a constitution, which they joyfully received. Had they been without this leadership the country would have been torn by rivalries of various parties contending for supremacy. But accustomed for centuries to look to the throne for guidance, and distrust any lesser authority, the people almost without exception loyally followed the Emperor's lead and within the short space of eighty years have adjusted themselves harmoniously to the conditions imposed by our modern forms of civilisation.

Keeping in mind this trait of Japanese psychology we can trace and understand the development of the art of flower arrangement from its position as the pastime of an individual in the Imperial Court in the sixth century to the prized accomplishment of the masses of the twentieth century.

During the six centuries which elapsed between the beginning of flower arrangement in what is known as the Suiko Period and the establishment of a military dictatorship at Kamakura in the twelfth century, all forms of culture flourished, with the Imperial Court, first at Nara, later at Kyoto, as the centre and fountain-head. The many forms of Chinese civilisation became modified and changed ; Chinese literature was studied and used as a model for Japanese literature which made rapid advancement. Japanese architecture was modified by Chinese ideas, gardens took on their present form and flower arrangement developed into an art practised not only by the priests and court nobles, but by all the feudal nobility. The Heian Period, or the Period of Peace, from the eighth to the twelfth century, was a time of great luxury for the Imperial Court and all its followers ; elegance in food and clothing and dwelling houses was the controlling idea ; luxury and extravagance reached an extreme degree. Painting and poetry contests were held in the court, and flower-viewing festivals were indulged in by both court and people. A favourite pastime of the lords of that time was the *Kyokusui-no-en* or " Feast of the Winding Stream," held in the great gardens in celebration of the blossoming of special flowers or when the maple was at its best. The nobles, attired in gorgeous robes and attended by their ladies in equally splendid garb, disposed themselves about the garden on the banks of the little stream without which no garden was complete. Well provided with *saké*, the national wine, they waited while a tiny *saké* cup, red lacquered and bearing the theme for a poem, floated down stream to them. Then, quaffing the beverage, they composed a poem. Or sometimes the proceedings varied : a cup brimming full of *saké* was set afloat and the players of this most aesthetic game wrote a poem, extolling the beauty of the flower in whose honour the meeting was held, before the cup with its contents reached them.

The love of flowers was carried to extravagant lengths, some even going to the extent of covering trees with artificial flowers in the Winter to produce the illusion of Summer, or of covering distant hills with white cloth to simulate snow in the Summer, for snow-viewing is counted as a " Flower Festival " in this beauty-loving land.

One of the earliest forms of arrangements was called *Shin-no-hana*. These were floral compositions arranged about a central or *Shin* branch. In a personal interview with one connected with the old original school of flower arrangement it was ascertained that these earliest arrangements were triangular in general outline and consisted of three main branches as they do to-day.

At first confined to religious purposes only, flower arrangement soon came into vogue as a decoration for the Imperial Court. It must be noted here that while many of the Japanese Emperors (*Tenno*) were encouragers of Buddhism, and in that capacity made use of the Buddhist style of flower arrangement, in their official capacity as head of the Japanese nation they participated in *Shinto* rites, never Buddhist. Floral offerings in a *Shinto* ceremony consist of branches of *sakaki*, a glossy evergreen leaf, only—flowers are not used. The gorgeous-coloured artfully arranged floral compositions developed under the influence of Buddhism were used as secular decorations in the court. Fostered by the prosperity of the Buddhist movement in Japan, a very ornate and complicated form of arrangement was developed. These were known as *Rikka* and were constructed of pine and other evergreens together with bright coloured blossoms. They stand six feet or more in height and require days to complete. Sen-ke—twelfth master of the *Ike-no-bo*

14

line of teachers, who died in the middle of the eleventh century, published the first written treatise on *Rikka*. An alternative reading for *Rikka* is *Tatebana* or " Standing Flowers." During the luxurious Heian Period (794–1159) the making of these arrangements became a pastime of the court nobles.

Rikka arrangements are intended to suggest or symbolise a bit of natural scenery. Plant materials were (and still are) used to represent different natural objects ; rocks and stones are symbolised by pine branches and the waters of a river or small stream by white chrysanthemums ; but the water of the sea is left to the viewer's imagination. These landscapes were copied from nature and very often modelled from a black and white landscape picture. Difficult to make, these arrangements are seldom seen ; only those very efficient in the art dare attempt their construction. Perfected by the masters of the *Ike-no-bo* school at Kyoto these have become almost exclusively their prerogative. Side by side with this elaborate form of arrangement existed another and comparatively simpler form, termed *Sashi-bana*, or *Heika*, sometimes translated as " Vase Flowers." These arrangements were used to decorate the dwelling houses, or in celebration of flower festivals.

The Heian Period was an era of refined and effeminate amusements and one result of such conditions was the growing disinclination of the court and feudal nobility to proceed to distant posts in discharge of their administrative duties. Gradually there grew up the practice of deputy administrators, and the administrative power fell from the relaxed hands of the hereditary nobles into the more aggressive hands of the military nobility. But the court at Kyoto, given over to the pursuit of aesthetic pastimes, continued to be the centre and fountain-head of all culture. To avoid this enervating and softening influence Yoritomo, chief of the feudal lords and

15

virtual military dictator, established his *Baku-fu*, or camp government, at Kamakura.

It might be supposed that the growth of a military administration would mean the suppression of the arts—but such was not the case. The military men, faced with the task of administering the laws as well as guarding the country, felt the need of a form of religion simple enough for camp life yet profound enough to inspire and invigorate the mind, and found this help in *Zen* Buddhism. The aim of *Zen* training is to overcome the worries of the world and attain poise of mind and strength of character, and the test of attainment in *Zen* is found in a moral life. In this spiritual training, the ethical principle is associated with aesthetic refinement, and aesthetic refinement is regarded not only as a means for the composure of the mind but as a natural expression of the soul deriving its poise and peace from the bosom of the universe. This combination of moral life with the sense of beauty was the basis of *Bushido*, the Way of the Warrior. This phase of teaching of the great Indian master, although developed in China, in Japan took on the colouring of the Japanese mentality, and has become so intimate a part of the Japanese life that to-day it is difficult to determine whether certain aspects are due to its influence or are innately Japanese.

To meet the need of a quiet place for study and meditation the *tokonoma*, originally known as *oshi-ita*, was evolved. This was an alcove in the room that faced the garden in which was hung a wall-hanging, and on the floor of which an ornament or incense burner and a flower arrangement were placed. This wall-hanging consisted usually of a landscape in monochrome or a beautifully written bit of calligraphy expressive of some deep ethical teaching. As *tatami*, or mats, came into more general use,

16

A good example of how the principles of flower arrangement control
the composition of groups of shrubbery in a garden. The
positions of Shin-Soe-Tai are easily discernible.

the floor of the *oshi-ita* was covered with a mat and from then on this alcove became known as the *tokonoma*. *Zen* places great emphasis on the affinity of man's soul with nature ; and is essentially a teaching that encourages communion with nature ; it affected not only homes and gardens, but flower arrangements as well. Flower arrangements which had reflected the luxurious and elegant life of the court in size and shape, became modified and simplified by the ideas of naturalism and simplicity inculcated by *Zen* teachings.

Down to the establishment of the Kamakura Government at the end of the twelfth century, *Rikka* continued to be the dominant form of arrangement. Until this time the Indian idea of gorgeous and elaborate design held sway over the art of flower arrangement, but now came a change, a simplification or Japonisation of all arts ; flower arrangement felt this influence and *Ike-bana* or " Living Flowers " took its present shape.

Yoshimasa, Eighth Shogun of the Ashikaga line (1143—1472), although head of a great military clique, was a generous patron of all the arts and protector and encourager of artists. It was under his administration that the tea-ceremony, or *Cha-no-yu*, was perfected. Flower arrangement is so intricately bound up with *Cha-no-yu* that a few words must be devoted to its explanation.

In itself but the simple serving of a cup of tea in harmonious surroundings, this tea ceremony influenced every phase of Japanese life. For its performance even the style of dwelling houses was altered, gardens were designed, materials woven, utensils created, and pictures painted. Based on the *Zen* teachings of the unity of all life and the harmony of man and nature, its influence extended from the Imperial Court down to the trades people, for during the peaceful and prosperous times of the Tokugawa Shogunate even

19

they studied this art. Flower arrangement under its influence took on the form known as *Cha-bana*, or "Tea Flower," often an austere and simple arrangement of one flower and its leaves, or a spray of flowering shrub in the most natural manner ; *Cha-bana* expresses perfectly the spirit of the tea ceremony.

The term *Nageire* seems to have come into use about the same time as that of *Cha-bana*. It is an alternative name for *Sashi-bana* and was applied to small natural arrangements used for decorative purposes. It is a free unstudied arrangement and unlike *Ike-bana* which emphasises beauty of line and form *Nageire* strives to express the nature of the flower used.

There is an interesting anecdote in connection with the origin of the term *Nageire*. It is said that Taiko Hideyoshi, one of the greatest generals that Japan has had, and one who recognised no limit to his ambitions, but who set out to conquer China by way of Korea, was one hot summer day engaged in the subjugation of Odawara, a rebellious province. Because of the heat he had caused a vessel of water to be placed near him to cool the air. In attendance on him was his favourite tea master Sen-no-Rikyu, whom he idly ordered to arrange some irises which were growing in a field near-by. Rikyu without hesitation plucked a flower, added some leaves to it, then drawing a small knife from its place in the sheath of his sword, he tied it to the flower with a leaf and flung it into the vessel of water where it stood upright. Hideyoshi exclaimed, " How cleverly your throw-in (*nageire*) took position just now ! "

Yoshimasa himself made a study of the method known as *Sho-getsu-do*, a branch of *Ike-no-bo* which still exists. Kobori Enshu, tea master and art connoisseur, regretted that so little record had been kept of the different methods of flower arrangement and commissioned a tea master, Ippo, to formulate a set of rules for arranging flowers for the tea ceremony. This Ippo school of flower arrangement became merged into the teaching and a mere part of the Kobori school of *Cha-no-yu*. The Enshu school of to-day has no connection with Kobori Enshu, but was started about the same time by a priest of a Nichiren temple, Honshosai Ittoku, in Tokyo, then known as Edo. At this time the term *Ike-bana* was not used so much as *Sashi-bana* because the flowers were forced into a holder.

Modern *Nageire* is a free natural arrangement of flowers apparently carelessly placed in a container but actually conforming to all the old art canons. *Moribana*—" piled up flowers "—is much the same. Sometimes the two seem to merge into one another and into the older school of *Ike-no-bo*, but in general *Moribana* is arranged in low flat containers, *Nageire* in deep containers, and *Ike-no-bo* in the traditional containers ; the exceptions are the *Ike-no-bo* arrangement of *omoto*, see page 159, which resembles *Moribana*, and the hanging *Ike-no-bo* arrangements which resemble *Nageire*.

Included under the classification of *Ike-bana* is a type of arrangement of fruit, vegetables and flowers with roots attached arranged in a wooden leaf-shaped or black lacquered tray.

Until the time of Yoshimasa, the end of the fifteenth century, the school of arrangement known as *Ike-no-bo* seems to have held sway. It was Yoshimasa who granted the master of the school, Senjun, twenty-sixth in unbroken line from Ono-no-Imoko, the title of *Dai Nippon Kado no Iemoto,* or " Originator of the Art of Japanese Flower Arrangement." With the wider diffusion of culture and the growth of the different schools of tea ceremony other schools of flower arrangement came into being, some of which have disappeared, but many of which continue to-day. These other schools made some slight modifications in the arrangements but none of them departed very widely in actual form ; the difference between schools lies mostly in the terms applied to branches and the teaching symbolised by them.

While each successive teacher of the *Ike-no-bo* school makes his contribution to its accumulation of floral lore, still to the unpractised eye there is very little difference between the arrangements of to-day and those of a hundred years ago, or two or three hundred. During the peaceful time of the Tokugawa Shogunate flower arrangement prospered ; and masters of the Rokkakudo were summoned to arrange flowers for Shogun and Emperor. From being the pastime of priests and court nobles *Ike-bana* became an accomplishment of all classes of people and by the time of the Meiji Restoration few and poor were the households where there was not at least one member skilled in the making of these arrangements.

The inrush of Western civilisation, far from retarding the growth of this most impracticable art, has heightened it ; new

22

schools are springing into existence to meet the new requirements. The *Ike-no-bo* arrangements hold their own ground (in fact that school is increasing in popularity) but as they continue to exhibit the old principles of religious association to some extent, they are considered suitable to be displayed only in the *tokonoma*, while other forms of arrangement based on the old principles are being developed for Western style rooms where a *tokonoma* is not available.

Our readers have no doubt noticed that throughout the entire history of flower arrangement no woman's name appears. In literature women played a prominent part, especially in the development of a purely Japanese style at the time when Chinese literature and learning threatened its existence. Many of the best known Japanese poets were women, and Murasaki Shikibu's novel, the *Genji Monogatari*, or "Tales of the Genji," written in the eleventh century, has never been surpassed in any language. But in flower arrangement, as in the tea ceremony, men played the part of leaders. There is no record of any outstanding woman master in all the long history of flower arrangement. It is an interesting peculiarity of the Japanese people that the arts for centuries have been in the hands of the *samurai*, the military men of the nation. Strange phenomenon—a country in the grip of a rigid military oligarchy enjoying peace and the practice of the arts to an almost unbelievable degree ! For while the Imperial Court at Kyoto continued to engage in its undeviating pursuit of all forms of art and literature, it was the military men who were the agents for diffusing this culture throughout the masses of the people. During the peaceful and prosperous times of the Tokugawa Shogunate even the trades people felt the influence of *Bushido*, and the tea ceremony and flower arrangement became part of their daily life. With the Meiji Restoration and the levelling of all class distinctions came the partial emancipation of woman from her old position of social inferiority and she began to emerge from the obscurity of the home into the public light. As the wife of a *samurai* and acting head of the household during his absence, woman had been trained in all the arts of the *samurai*, even to that of defending her home with arms, but always in the name of her lord and master ; now she has stepped forth in her own right. Many new schools of flower arrangement have women as their founders and there are recognised tea masters among them, though men continue to hold the highest positions in these two kindred arts.

Ike-no-bo, the oldest school of flower arrangement, is the basic school for all the countless other schools that have appeared and to-day it is substantially the same as it was over a thousand years ago both in shape and name and it continues to be the most popular of all the schools of flower arrangement.

At the end of the nineteenth century, as a result of the wave of Europeanisation that swept over Japan with the opening of her doors to foreign intercourse, a further modification of this traditional art took place. European houses began to supersede

24

the Japanese style homes ; a need was felt for a method of arranging flowers suitable for table decoration and equally decorative from any point of view ; and many new schools sprang into existence, some of which totally disregard the old principles, aesthetic as well as philosophic.   The best of these new schools, while they do not disregard the beauty of line inherent in the old schools, have developed a less restrained and formal type of arrangement. Modern *Nageire*, distinct from the *Nageire* of *Ike-no-bo*, came into use about seventy years ago, while the second modern type of arrangement, *Moribana*, dates back but thirty years.

Ike-no-bo was developed in Kyoto on the spot on which to-day stands the Rokkakudo (Six-sided Temple), and the descendants of the original teacher still live there and teach the art as it has been handed down to them by their forefathers.   All diplomas for this school, for whatever part of Japan, are issued by the master there, the forty-third in line from the founder.   Certain days each month he himself teaches and all devotees of *Ike-no-bo* who can, avail themselves of this privilege ; but this is not possible for all, so other ways have been contrived.

To the Japanese, the study of flower arrangement is a serious matter. Formerly to obtain a diploma from the *Ike-no-bo Iemoto* (*Ike-no-bo* Head House) the student of flower arrangement registered his name together with that of his teacher and he was expected to study from three to five years. At the end of that time, if he could pass an examination before properly qualified judges who were sent out from Kyoto, he might receive the much coveted diploma of efficiency in this art.

According to the usual Japanese method of teaching any art, the pupil was set to making an arrangement guided by very terse instructions from the master ; and he continued to make this one arrangement until he had not only acquired manual dexterity in the making of this particular composition but had glimpsed the reason behind the master's instructions. When the teacher recognised that the pupil had reached this point he divulged to him certain so-called secrets or *kaden*.

Often these *kaden* were merely rules of proportion or certain methods of preserving and expressing the natural growing habit of some particular plants which the teacher had learned by years of experience. Teacher and pupils sharing these *kaden*, or secret instructions, formed a sort of secret society.

But the era of speed shows itself even in the practice of flower arrangement ; some of the more progressive teachers of to-day have read the signs of the times and have formulated their teachings systematically so that even the merest tyro can grapple intelligently with this fascinating art. Recognising the fact that most foreigners (and an ever-increasing number of Japanese) have not years to devote to any art, certain enterprising *Ike-no-bo* teachers of Tokyo have obtained an exception to this rule. The pupil may register his name as well as his teacher's, who must be one recognised at Kyoto, and at the end of one year he may undergo

Annual gathering of teachers of one of the modern schools of flower arrangement in Tokyo. These meetings are devoted to a serious discussion of the work accomplished during the year and plans for the future.

Mrs. Josui Oshikawa, "Iemoto" or Founder of the modern school of flower arrangement, Sho-fu-ryu, and co-author of this book, seated in the position of guest of honour before the tokonoma.

examination.   It is understood that he devotes himself intensively to the study.   As yet but few foreigners have availed themselves of this opportunity.

The school illustrated in this book is the *Sho-fu-ryu*, dating back to the first efforts to adapt the traditional *Ike-no-bo* to the uses of foreign-style buildings.   *Sho-fu-ryu* is a happy combination of traditional principles of flower arrangement and certain time honoured garden artifices.   Its name translates " Pine Breeze " and its arrangements strive to express a spirit of naturalness, as natural and as effortless as the wind in the pines on a Summer day.

Sho-fu-ryu is one of the most popular of the modern schools and appeals especially to the European because of its clever adaptation of the old principles to new conditions.   The founder of *Sho-fu-ryu*, uncle of the Japanese collaborator of this book, was a *samurai* well versed in the art and literature of Japan.   As a young man he came in contact with some of the earliest Europeans to settle in this country.   He saw that the traditional formal arrangements were suited neither to the foreign type of architecture, nor to the European mentality.   But he also realised that the old art principles were not to be lightly cast off, and that they could be adapted to the needs of Europeans and contribute to their aesthetic life.

Retaining the three basic groups of *Shin-Soe-Tai* which in the traditional *Ike-no-bo* arrangements suggest one living unit, he added *Mikoshi* and *Tome*, two garden artifices, to widen out the composition and to make it less formal and so more suitable for Europeans and those Japanese who live in European houses.

True to the teaching of *Ike-no-bo*, *Sho-fu-ryu* stresses beauty of line ; leaves and even blossoms are sacrificed to this end but joy in the finished composition increases with continued association.

29

A properly composed *Sho-fu-ryu* arrangement shows both fluidity of line and fidelity to the natural growth of the plant used.

Anyone may set up his or her own school of flower arrangement if he can attach to himself sufficient followers. With the change of national capital from Kyoto to Tokyo came a corresponding shifting of culture and most of the new schools of flower arrangement have originated here. Teachers of flower arrangement, and there are thirty thousand of them in Tokyo alone, are under the jurisdiction of the Board of Education and founders of new schools (*Iemoto*) must be recognised by it. They are granted a certificate stating that they have complied with the requirements of the Board and are licensed to grant teachers' diplomas. At all the big conventions of teachers of *Ike-bana* a representative of this Board attends. To-day in Tokyo there are about thirty well-known schools, both old and new. In all Japan there are perhaps five hundred or more fairly large schools of which number only about one hundred are recognised by the Board of Education.

FLOWERS IN JAPANESE LIFE

THE Japanese word *hana*, the only English equivalent for which is "flowers," means much more than the English word, for it includes not only all tree foliage but reeds and grasses. What we understand by the word "flowers" is termed *kusa bana*—"grass flowers"—in Japanese, and *kusa bana* form but a small part of the material used in a flower arrangement. Slender branches of almost any tree or bush, flowering or ever-green, are used either alone or in conjunction with cut flowers.

33

Reeds and grasses are favourite materials for flower compositions, especially in Autumn.

Ike-bana, or the art of flower arrangement, makes use of tree branches, grasses and flowers to produce a lineal composition of great beauty—highly artificial but at the same time much influenced by consideration of the natural growing habit and life rhythm of the plant material used. Mere blossoms are ruthlessly sacrificed for beauty of line ; and while bending is resorted to in some cases, plant material which naturally grows stiff and straight is not tampered with but arranged in conformity with that growing habit.

The Japanese seldom use a full-blown flower in their arrangements ; they make their arrangements of buds so that they may have the pleasure of seeing them open into blossoms. The use of the Japanese method gives the arranger more pleasure than the Western method. It is self evident that an arrangement of buds, which will expand into beauty, will give pleasure longer than one of flowers ready to droop and die.

The outstanding characteristic of a Japanese flower arrangement is its naturalness and suggestion of growth ; it appears to be a flourishing group of growing shrubs and flowers, never a collection of wilting flowers detached from the parent stem as do so many Western bouquets arranged without regard to the life-rhythm of the flower used.

The Japanese can, with a few reeds and a handful of field flowers, recall a walk into the country-side, or with an arrangement of pine branches and chrysanthemums suggest a wish for continued peace and tranquillity.

That the practice of *Ike-bana* is widespread is proved by the frequency of public exhibits of arrangements, not only in the large cities, but all over the country. Poor and mean indeed is the

An exhibit of a modern school of flower arrangement held in one of the large downtown department stores. Such displays are quite frequent and attract crowds of visitors.

village that does not at times have such an exhibit, while in Tokyo scarcely a day passes that there is not a public exhibit somewhere, other than the many private ones held by teachers and pupils much as recitals are given by our piano and singing teachers. No young woman's education is considered complete without some knowledge of this art.

Factories employing hundreds of girls, department stores and even large restaurants furnish competent teachers for their employees and allow them time off for the lessons. Government offices encourage their women workers to study this art by providing teachers and allowing them to use the government buildings for lessons. Lessons on flower arrangement are broadcast over the radio frequently, while one of the charms of Japanese life is the weekly gathering of the neighbourhood women folk, old and young, rich and poor, in a democratic meeting at the home of their teacher, to practise flower arrangement under her guidance.

Another rather unique manifestation of the use of flower arrangement is the setting forth of formal arrangements along the streets through which the *O-Mikoshi*, or " god-car," makes its way in the annual festivals observed by all shrines, for the pleasure of the god or *kami* who rides in it. Those living in houses fronting on these streets display their arrangements within the opened fronts of their homes while those not so favourably situated join together and transform an empty building or metamorphose a commonplace store into a garden, where the art of man contends in friendly rivalry with the natural beauty of nature.

It is interesting to note also that while there is not the least suggestion of monotony, for no two arrangements are ever exactly alike, still the shape of the arrangement no matter where

37

found, in the furthermost south or uttermost north, in great cities or small villages, is in general the same.

Professor Masaharu Anesaki of the Imperial University says that Japanese literature abounds in short stories and legends " all based on the popular belief that flowers are endowed with souls not unlike the human soul," so it is not surprising that every year in Tokyo, on the 8th of April, there is a Buddhist ceremony for the repose of the souls of the flowers used throughout the year. A miniature altar is erected of fresh flowers and green bamboo and before it bands of gaily dressed children, wearing golden crowns and carrying blossoms, weave about in the intricate steps of an ancient Buddhist dance while solemn musicians play weird music on old instruments. A sight to please even the souls of flowers.

Flower-viewing excursions, or *hanami*, are indulged in by all classes of people, rich and poor, young and old. By train, by motor car, on foot or on the backs of the more sturdy members of the family, all flock to well-known beauty spots to see the blossoms. Special trains are run and rates to different points reduced ; and hard-hearted indeed is the master who will not give his little

A class of young girls practising flower arrangement at the home of their teacher.

A night class in flower arrangement in one of the Municipal Neighbourhood
Welfare Association Halls. These girls are employed
in various offices during the day.

kozo (apprentice boy) a day off to view the cherry blossoms. Great factories send their girl employees in groups of a hundred at a time and schools suspend classes when the blossoms are at their best.

But it must not be thought that it is only the cherry that lures its admirers into pilgrimage ; the plum, the peony, the iris, the lotus, the maple, all have their followers.

In Tokyo there are peony gardens with plants a hundred years old bearing blossoms of unbelievable size and richness in colouring, carefully tended by gardeners whose fathers before them tended the same plants. These are private gardens but, in conformity with a typically Japanese spirit of democracy, during the week that the blossoms are at their best they are thrown open to the public, which does not hesitate to avail itself of the privilege. Official count of the visitors to the iris gardens of the Meiji Shrine gave forty thousand as one day's total ; this garden, once the favourite retreat of the Emperor Meiji's consort, is closed to the public except at this time. The irises here grow to a height of four and five feet, of all colours and kinds, and as they sway and wave in the wind

41

one no longer wonders why most of their names refer to dances or dancers.

Not so popular with the general public but appreciated by a select few is the early morning visit to a lotus pond to hear the buds break into blossom as the sun rises. However, to be abroad so early in lotus blossom time is no hardship; for these flowers bloom in the hottest season of the year and the early morning breeze is almost as delightful as the view.

None but the Japanese have ever considered snow-viewing as a flower festival, but such it is considered by them. It must be remembered that the custom of including snow among flowers originated in Kyoto where snow is comparatively unusual and lasts but a few hours. A more beautiful sight than a Japanese landscape under a light mantle of snow is difficult to imagine.

Their gardens, too, are designed to show to good advantage in the snow. On a wintry morning, when all sound is hushed by a light fall of snow, a Japanese garden with its contrast of colours, the brilliant green of the *nanten's* glossy leaves and its red berries,

42

Moribana and Nageire arrangements at one of the many public exhibits in Tokyo.

Flowers are brought daily to the door of even the humblest homes. Such flower carts as this are to be seen in the residential districts of all big cities both in winter and in summer. The venders make their rounds quite early in the morning.

the rocks showing stark and black and the sombre green of the pine trees, is a picture long retained by the lover of the beautiful.

The love of flowers is not confined to the Japanese people, it is true, but it is equally true that there are few other people in the world to-day with whom the love of flowers plays such an important part in their daily lives ; and they are the only people who have elevated the technique of flower arrangement to the dignity of an art.

Flowers are brought to the doors of even the humblest of homes and a housewife's first duty is to offer fresh flowers before the tablet of the ancestors. The construction of a suitable arrangement is as necessary a preparation for the entertainment of a guest as is the preparation of suitable food.

In a big city like Tokyo hardly a week passes without an exhibit of flower arrangements in one of the downtown stores, or in the great municipal art gallery. One of the exhibits of 1935, that of a single school, the *Sho-fu-ryu*, lasted for a week and over three hundred arrangements were entered. Another in which a hundred different schools participated had over nineteen hundred entries. Contrary to what might be expected the Japanese are

45

content with the simplest of natural blooms for these exhibits; flowers out of season or forced blooms are not prized as in other countries. For the largest and most important exhibits only flowers in season are used; the most famous teacher and his humblest pupil will arrange the same materials. The commoner the material, the greater the skill required for a beautiful arrangement.

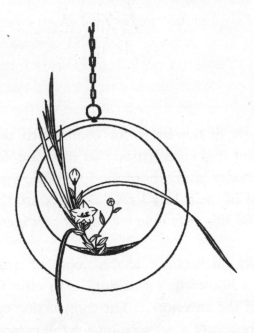

Because the masters of Japanese flower arrangement consider their efforts an expression of art, they are not over-concerned with the selection of plant material. Contrary to the Western idea of depending on beauty of material for a beautiful arrangement, they take pride in making a beautiful composition of commonplace materials. One thing they demand: the material must be fresh; wilted leaves and drooping flowers are an abomination to them. With very few exceptions, full-blown flowers are never used.

46

Also flowers forced to blossom out of season are not admired. Japanese flower arrangement aims to express within the house, by means of seasonal material, the greater life of nature without ; and it is this spirit, this idea of beauty in the commonplace, that is of value to the Western world.

On first consideration it might seem that having definite principles and set rules for the construction of floral compositions would result in stiff and stereotyped arrangements, but actually the Japanese use these rules and principles as unconsciously as does the Western artist working with his chosen art medium. It is only for the purpose of introducing the idea of flowers as an art medium to the Western world that the authors of this book have thought it necessary to draw attention to the universality of all art principles, and to stress the mechanics of the art of flower arrangement.

To the Japanese, more important than the rules governing the proportions of an arrangement is the fact that a flower arrangement must express both the individuality of the arranger and the life rhythm of the plant. Often an arrangement, highly artificial in construction and actually not conforming to laws of growth, suggests vividly the feeling of natural growth. A Japanese flower arrangement aims at a presentation of an idealised type of natural growth rather than a faithful copy of nature.

Japanese flower arrangements are designed to be viewed from one position and this at first seems strange to Western thought, but a moment's consideration will serve to recall the fact that any work of art, whether painting or statuary, is designed to be looked at from one point of vantage. Incorrect hanging has ruined the effect of many a good painting and, with rare exceptions, no statue is equally pleasing viewed from all sides. Why should we expect of an artistic arrangement of flowers what we do not expect of an artistic arrangement of other materials?

But there is another contributing cause for this one-sidedness of floral arrangement. It is almost an impossibility for a Japanese to disregard the natural law of growth, though he loves to accentuate the effect of these laws. There is no tree or flower that naturally grows equally to the North and South ; instinctively plants turn to the sun. The Japanese have merely accentuated this idea to produce a thing of beauty. Even the most ultra modern schools of arrangement which repudiate all the old traditions of aesthetic teachings and ostentatiously use the square or the circle for general outline and delight in even numbers, even they hesitate to face their flowers in all directions. Almost unconsciously they follow natural laws of growth in their arrangements.

The objection is sometimes raised that the set formal way of Japanese flower arrangement, especially the *Ike-no-bo*, is not suitable for our Western houses. This is true in many homes, where a more informal friendly arrangement is suitable ; in that case a *Nage-ire* or *Moribana* arrangement is best. But in the more modern type of homes, where elegant simplicity is the keynote, no other method of flower arrangement is as appropriate.

However, the idea of greatest value to the Western world is the idea of living flowers. A properly composed flower arrangement, either of the *Ike-no-bo* or *Sho-fu-ryu* schools, is not only a thing of beauty, but an expression of life—it appears to be a friendly group of growing plants, not a collection of dying blooms, as too often the Western bouquets are. The Western method of selecting blossoms just at the point of perfection, cutting them all at one length and then crowding them into a vase in an attitude expressive only of a lack of strength and confusion produces only a sense of pity in the Japanese mind.

Try the experiment yourself :—Take three roses and place them in the usual manner in a glass vase, heavy heads hanging and leaves in a confused mass with stems crossing at all angles in the water. Now take a low soft green pottery bowl and place a small holder

in it. Take time to examine your roses ; determine which side of
the leaves is glossiest, and find the angle at which the stems will
hold the weight of the blossoms, as the Japanese say, "so as to catch
the dew." Take a bud if possible, or a half-opened flower, and
cut it once and a half to twice the diameter of your vase ; cut the
flower that is fullest blown one-third the height of this and cut the
third flower two-thirds the height of the first one. Now insert
the roses one at a time upright in the holder, the longest directly
upright, with its flower reaching upwards, not drooping ; insert
the second longest by the side of the first, but lean it a little away
from that one ; add the shortest on the opposite side of the tallest
and a little separate from the first two, leaning away from them at
quite an angle, but be sure that the blossoms face up, not down.
A little practice will teach you how to balance a heavy-headed
flower.

Now compare the two arrangements. The first arrangement
is a group of blossoms waiting to die, suggestive of nothing but
the power of man to force nature to do his bidding, to produce
perfection of form and colouring. The second arrangement shows

three vital blossoms, each leaf instinct with life, stems emerging from the surface of the water as if from one root ; the whole thing a growing plant—suggestive of the power of nature to produce beauty. You have brought within the walls of your home a suggestion of the vital force of all nature.

The spirit of a Japanese flower arrangement is to make a thing of beauty out of commonplace materials. No shrub is too rugged, nor flower too humble to be used.

To the student of flower arrangement we would say : Do not be content merely to copy the arrangements pictured in this book. Study your own natural floral surroundings and seek to express them in your arrangements ; or call to remembrance childhood gardens or well-loved picnic spots and use them as the theme of your floral compositions. This book will have been written in vain if it does no more than spread a stereotyped form of flower arrangement over the world. Its purpose is to set forth the fundamental principles which have guided and controlled the development of Japanese flower arrangement and which, if adhered to in other countries, will produce a type of arrangement expressive of such countries, not of Japan. A Japanese flower arrangement is a miniature, or rather a suggestion, of the gardens of Japan. Japan abounds in beautiful scenery, the country-side is green the year around and Japanese gardens are designed to represent this scenery. Unlike the Western gardens, no flowers are grown in them ; their only purpose is to suggest the mountains, hills and valleys of the country. In countries not so favoured by nature a different type of garden has been evolved and the flower arrangements of such countries should suggest or picture the gardens known and loved by the people of those countries.

51

LOVE OF NATURE—SYMBOLISM—LINE

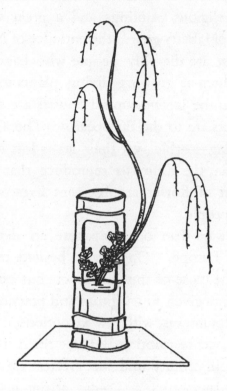

IKE-BANA, or the art of flower arrangement in Japan, is the development of centuries and to understand this art three fundamental characteristics of the Japanese mentality must be kept in mind : an innate love of nature and all its manifestations, an equally instinctive love of symbolism and a love of line in all forms of art expression. · Much as the Japanese love the visible forms of nature they are not content with them but must forever search for the inner and hidden meaning of those forms. The idea of expressing

philosophical or religious concepts by some form of art is not un-
known to the people of other countries. European museums are
crowded with religious paintings and a great stone reproduction
of the Goddess of Liberty guards the entrance of New York harbour.
But the Japanese are the only people who have chosen so perish-
able an art medium as growing, living plants to express ideas and
aspirations. To the Japanese mind flowers are as acceptable an art
medium as paints are to the European. The Greeks carved their
ideals in enduring marble, yet their art is lost to the world ; only
fragments remain, the ability to reproduce that art is gone. But
in Japan the art of flower arrangement lives on—a vital force in
the life of the people.

In more ways than one, Japanese art developed differently
from the art of Europe. One would hesitate to say that the love
of nature was the cause of this difference, but certain it is that very
little attention was given to sculpture and practically none to genre
painting. Sculpture was, with few exceptions, confined to religious
representations ; genre painting did not reach its full development
until the sixteenth century and the greatest masters of that school
produced many landscapes. To-day at the annual exhibits at the
Ueno Art Gallery, barring the atrocious, so-called " foreign style "
nudes, flower and nature themes greatly predominate. A favourite
form of Japanese art is the *sumi-ye* or " line drawing in Indian
ink," without colour, but showing a remarkable mastery of line.
Even in the better known *ukiyo-ye* (Japanese prints), strength
and beauty of line were more important to their designers than
colour.

The Japanese love of line, a characteristic shared by all
Orientals, is everywhere manifest but especially in their architecture. The roof lines of their houses are among the most beauti-

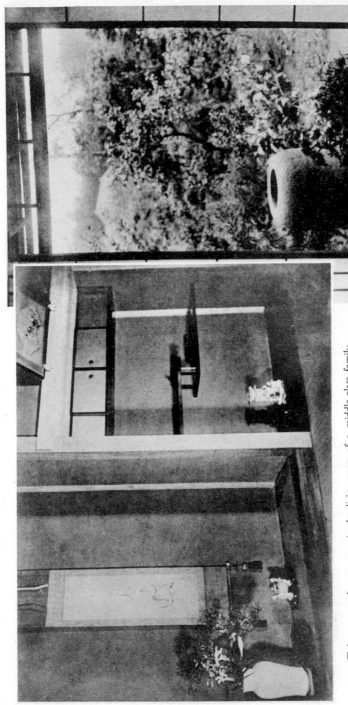

Tokonoma and ornaments in the living room of a middle-class family. Note the irregular triangle formed by the figure in the wall hanging, the vase of flowers and the ornament in the right hand section of the alcove, illustrating the application of the principles of flower arrangement to the placing of ornaments in a home.

View of garden from the interior of the house with dwarf trees in the foreground.

ful in the world. Both interiorly and exteriorly the lines of timber construction are not only not hidden, but emphasised. The *torii*, that essentially Japanese development of the gate, seen before all *Shinto* shrines, is unpainted, unpretentious, depending on line for its beauty; but few people having once seen it ever forget the charm of its silhouette against the sky. This love of line has been fostered for centuries; even the garments are influenced by it and flower arrangement did not escape. Far greater stress is placed on beauty of line than on harmony of colour. A Japanese flower arrangement of the old school consists of three main branches (or groups of branches) joined at the base and presenting the appearance of a living growing unit, an arrangement in which grace and beauty of line play the most important part.

The Japanese consider a line more expressive than a solid or plane, for a line has the latent possibility of becoming a plane which in turn may develop into a solid. It is said that the book of nature is written in characters of geometry, and that for the study of material things, number, order and position are the three-fold clue to exact knowledge; this gives us the key to the use of the set triangular form gradually developed by the Buddhist priests to express their teachings.

The literal translation of the names applied to the three main branches of the *Ike-no-bo* school of arrangement, the oldest in existence and one with a history of over thirteen hundred years, throws light on the philosophical ideas held by the Japanese. The highest and central branch, about which all others take their respective positions, is called *Shin*. *Shin* can be written in more than one way, but the character originally used by the founder of this school, Ono-no-Imoko, is read " spiritual truth." The intermediate branch was designated *Soe*, then and now read " harmoniser " ; while the third and lowest branch is *Tai* or " material substance." These terms, first used thirteen hundred years ago, are still in use to-day. The originator of this form of art attempted with flowers to symbolise the part played by the love of nature and its manifestations as the harmoniser between spirit and matter.

The triangular form, the use of an odd number of branches,

the orientation of the composition to the points of the compass, all are capable of various interpretations and various interpretations have been ascribed to each and all. The influence of Confucian teachings can be traced in the use of the terms *Ten-Chi-Jin* or " Heaven-Earth-Man," for the three cardinal points. Reflecting the present world tendency to nationalism, Japan is now experiencing a revival of old national and spiritual cultures. This movement can be traced in the flower schools of to-day. The three main branches of the more modern schools are designated *Tenno* or " Emperor," *chichihaha* or " father and mother," and *kodomo* or " children." Actually there is very little difference in the terms used by the different schools ; for the *Tenno* (Emperor) is the embodiment of spiritual truth, *Shin*, and the representative of heaven, *ten*, on earth in the Japanese political philosophy. The Japanese *Tenno* has always held an unique position in the minds of his people ; he is the head and heart of the country. Just as the main branch of the arrangement, call it what you will, determines the size and shape of the arrangement and binds all its component parts into unity and harmony, so the *Tenno*, by right of his position as head of the great family state of Japan, strengthens and holds into unity the people of Japan. This teaching is not new, called into being to meet a present emergency, but is as old as the country itself.

The use of the triangle as a principle of art composition is not confined to Japan ; it is known to students the world over. No two flower arrangements are ever alike, for not only are no two flowers ever the same, but also the basis of their composition, the triangle, is capable of infinite variation.

The Japanese, when they set out to make a flower arrangement, have in mind a totally different concept of flowers from that held

61

by Westerners. To the Westerner, flowers are a symbol of luxury, they are loved for their colour, their scent, for their very perishableness. None of these things appeals to the Japanese. There are no people on the earth who enjoy the present moment more than the Japanese, but they want to be surrounded by objects which suggest permanent eternal ideas. To them " the grass of the field which to-day is and to-morrow is cast into the fire " is beautiful if contrasted with the pine tree, symbol of eternity. Their teaching for centuries has been that while this mortal life is short and fleeting, it is but a part of the universal life, and it is this eternal universal life that they are striving to express in all their art.

They are not content with merely beautiful things ; there must be some meaning behind the beauty, and to the expression of this hidden meaning much importance is attached. Flower arrangement for them is not only the arrangement of flowers for some decorative purpose, it is the picturing forth of some mental concept with flowers as the medium, and expressive of the arranger's individuality.

It seems almost impossible for the Japanese to enjoy flowers just as flowers. Never can it be said of them " a primrose by the river's brim a yellow primrose was to him ". There is hardly a flower or tree which has not some metaphysical or historical association, often both. Certain combinations of flowers are recognised immediately as suggestions of an old tradition, a fairy-tale, a poem or a wish.

In art and literature both, flower themes hold a prominent position, and the association of flowers with certain birds or animals is always observed. These combinations, originated in China, have become a fixed part of the Japanese cultural heritage and all are familiar with them and recognise them at once. The chagrin of a famous military leader when he failed to understand an allusion in a very obscure Chinese poem is the subject of one of the flower arrangements pictured in this book. See page 220.

Japanese interior architecture is severely simple in style—the construction timbers of a house are plainly visible, and there is but one place, the *tokonoma*, where ornaments may be displayed. Monotony is avoided by the frequent change of these ornaments and interest stimulated by the timeliness of the objects used and for this the flower arrangement is the key. Flowers out of season are seldom displayed and then only for a definite purpose. The size of the *tokonoma* necessarily varies with the size of the room, but no Japanese living room is complete without one, however simple. Because of the custom of keeping all household objects stored away in small closets shut off from the room, the average Japanese room is not more than twelve feet by fifteen and a room of that size will have an alcove of three feet by six. Often the entire end of a room is taken up by the *tokonoma* alcove and a set of shelves, also for display purposes.

A *tokonoma* is never crowded; three objects and no more are allowed at one time : a wall-hanging, a flower arrangement and a small metal or porcelain ornament, usually an incense burner. Quite frequently only the flower arrangement and wall-hanging are displayed. In any case all the objects are complementary one to the other. Suppose, a very obvious combination, a wall-hanging of a waterfall, the flower arrangement must consist of flowers that grow in or near water and the ornament must be a bronze fish or fisherman or some such object that is closely associated with water. Volumes could be written on this subject alone but we must content ourselves with a short list of the more common associations. A well-designed flower arrangement will never err in this regard.

The *tokonoma* is a result, not a cause, of flower arrangement. The development of this alcove was simultaneous with the spread of *Zen* teaching and although one group of scholars traces its origin to the bed place reserved for the *kami* or " superiors," the practice of *Zen* meditation which necessitates a place for a wall-hanging and a floral offering undoubtedly fostered its development. The *tokonoma* is built at right angles to the garden which in Japan is always to the south of the house, and a flower arrangement placed in the *tokonoma* would thus follow the natural laws of growth in reaching out to the sunlight. The *tokonoma* has lost its religious signification, but it is still reserved for formal flower arrangements and objects of art—nothing unclean or untidy is ever placed in it.

There is considerable etiquette observed in viewing a flower arrangement in a *tokonoma*, as there is with everything else in the daily life of the Japanese people. When a guest enters a room he is expected to admire the ornaments displayed for him. He should advance to within about three feet of the *tokonoma* where he should bow in recognition of the effort that his host has made to set forth a work of art. Then he should look first at the *kakemono*, or " wall-hanging " ; after pausing to appreciate that he should next look at the flower arrangement and compliment his host on his cleverness ; then, and not till then, he may remark on the beautiful flowers that have been used. The art with which the flowers are arranged is important, not the flowers themselves. Having properly complimented his host, he should bow again, this time in thanks, and return to his seat.

Great importance is attached to the selection of flowers for

View of tokonoma showing relation to garden, and the absence of all ornaments except those in the tokonoma.

A view of the garden of a small hotel. Note the old Japanese custom of placing blossoming flowers temporarily in the garden, to be removed when past their greatest beauty.

different occasions. For a visit of friendship the preference of the guest is considered, but for important occasions, such as weddings, funerals, anniversaries and festivals, tradition rules with an iron hand.

The chrysanthemum is perhaps the best loved of all the flowers. Asked to choose flowers for a flower arrangement, nine times out of ten a Japanese will select chrysanthemums. Chrysanthemums are available all the year and they are considered suitable for any occasion no matter how formal. At a flower arrangement exhibit in Tokyo not so long ago the place of honour was given to a hanging scroll on which was written in beautifully drawn characters a poetical expression of a wish for long life and happiness for the *Tenno* (Emperor) and before which was placed a modest arrangement of three sprays of small white chrysanthemums almost resembling daisies. To be sure, the vase they were arranged in was a priceless bronze made in China two thousand years ago and aged to a beautiful blue-green patina. Nothing less than an orchid would have been deemed suitable by a European, but to the Japanese that simple flower symbolised all that is grand and noble, dignified and beautiful, for in its conventionalised form it is the Imperial Crest of Japan. Further, it was a flower then growing in the gardens of the country. The Japanese share with the Russians a love of the very ground of their country and to them there is an inseparable bond between the land, the *Tenno* and themselves. So that those unassuming white flowers meant, to the one who arranged them and to the Japanese who viewed them, the natural God-bestowed symbol of the land that nourishes them, their *Tenno*, and themselves. It will be remembered that according to Japanese mythology the creator gods " gave birth " to both the islands of Japan and the forefathers of

69

Jimmu Tenno, First Emperor of Japan ; and every Japanese considers himself more or less distantly related to the ruler of his country. This idea of the relationship of land and people is difficult for the Occidental mind to grasp but it is a factor to be reckoned with in Japanese psychology.

The national flag of Japan is a red disc on a white ground ; termed by the Europeans the flag of the " rising sun ", by the Japanese themselves it is called the flag of the " origin of the sun," *Nippon no hata,* and to them the red disc of the sun and the sixteen petalled crest of the *Tenno* are interchangable. To find an analogy to this is not difficult ; Japan is not the only country in which the chrysanthemum is recognised as the symbol of the sun ; the very name by which this flower is known to Europeans, chrysanthemum, is a Greek word meaning " golden (the colour of the sun) flower."

Chrysanthemums came to Japan from China and were first cultivated during the Nara Period, some twelve hundred years ago according to the actual historical record, though some scholars claim they are indigenous to Japan. As early as the ninth century

70

the chrysanthemum was used as a crest but it was not until the nine-teenth century that it was made the exclusive prerogative of the *Tenno*. The chrysanthemum appears frequently as a motif in all forms of art, tapestry, lacquer ware, porcelains, etc., though never in its sixteen petalled form, which is reserved for the *Tenno*. When displayed in public places the sixteen petalled form is covered with a piece of paper to keep it from profanation by the public gaze.

In all forms of art the chrysanthemum is often represented in combination with flowing water, known as *kiku-sui*. This is an allusion to an old court festival, *Kyoku-sui-no-en*, or " the Feast of the Winding Stream." For its proper observance a great garden is necessary with a winding stream of water. It is said that in the twelfth century Kyoto had twelve such palace gardens to which the public were admitted on festival days. As with all other forms of culture, the love of chrysanthemums and their cultivation devel-oped in the Imperial Court and spread through the usual channels, the court nobles, the feudal nobles, the *samurai*, down to the people at large so that to-day even the ricksha-puller will have his pots of choice blooms which he tends lovingly throughout the year.

In chrysanthemum time in Tokyo displays of gorgeous blossoms appear in most unexpected places ; the humblest of shop keepers with no garden at all will proudly display one or two per-fect flowers which he has with much effort and loving care grown on his roof top ; and the policeman on the corner will surround his tiny bare box-like sentry house with masses of colour produced from nowhere as far as one can see. But it is at Ryogoku, a dis-trict in Tokyo, in a great building built primarily to house *sumo* or Japanese wrestling contests, that the chrysanthemum can be seen at its best.

Here every year are displayed *kiku-ningyo* or chrysanthemum dolls.   These dolls are life sized ; their heads, hands and feet are of some composition and startlingly lifelike, but their garments are made entirely of living chrysanthemums, so cunningly arranged that the figures appear to be clothed in tapestry and brocades. Such exhibits have been a feature of Tokyo life since the latter half of the eighteenth century, and to-day they can be seen in all the large cities of Japan.   Each year the characters portrayed and the backgrounds are different and for the month that they are on dis-play thousands visit them daily.   Besides the dolls the place is well worth visiting because of growing chrysanthemums such as can be found in any country.   Here can be seen single roots bearing, by actual count, hundreds of blossoms.   To such a degree of skill have the chrysanthemum fanciers reached that a single root has been made to bear two hundred and twelve blossoms, each blossom perfect and all of uniform size and shape, five inches in diameter. Also one may see plants grown in fantastic shapes, such as air-planes, autos, ships of good fortune and countless others.   How they manage to hold back some of the blossoms while they coax others to grow longer stems and then finally get them all to blossom simultaneously is a puzzle to the uninitiated.

Despite the fact that the Japanese can and do produce by arti-ficial means, that is in hothouses, great blooms such as are pro-duced by horticulturists in Europe and America, they never use them for flower arrangement, and even for exhibit purposes they judge them differently from the Westerner.   To receive considera-tion a plant must be perfect not only as to colour and size and shape of the blossom but as to the entire plant ; imperfect or badly spaced leaves will disqualify the most beautiful blossom.   For cut flowers for purposes of decoration for European style houses, im-ported varieties are grown by professional florists and sold in florist shops. But for flower arrangement small blossoms grown naturally in the open air are preferred ; two small villages to the north of Tokyo have for two hundred years supplied the Tokyo market.

The Feast of the Winding Stream of the Imperial Court is no longer observed. Its place has been taken by the Imperial Garden Party given by the *Tenno* to Japanese of prescribed rank and foreign dignitaries and diplomats, when the chrysanthemums are at their best in the Imperial gardens. The date of the old festival is commemorated on October 9th by the *Choyo-no-sekku*, Festival of Happiness, when every household in the land sets forth an arrangement of chrysanthemums and an appropriate hanging picture.

Shi-kunshi, or the Four Cultured Gentlemen, sometimes termed the Four Friends, is the name given to the combination in any form of art of the chrysanthemum with bamboo, plum blossom and the wild, or wood, orchid. It is a special favourite with designers of woven materials, sometimes set forth boldly and easily recognisable, at other times cleverly concealed and difficult to distinguish. In flower arrangement this combination is considered necessary for the proper celebration of any felicitous event. The orchid is loved for its purity because it unfolds its beauty in solitude. But it must not be thought that this Chinese orchid bears any resemblance to the gorgeous blooms found in most European florist shops. The flower of this wood orchid, while of surpassingly sweet odour, is almost totally lacking in colour. The plant is not prized for its colour but for the soft line of its leaves. The school of Japanese flower arrangement set forth in this book makes great use of this plant.

Flower arrangements of pine and chrysanthemums are to be found any time of the year, for almost any occasion. The Japanese love the contrast between the sturdy long-lived evergreen and the fragile blossoms ; to them the pine symbolises continuing vigorous life, the life which embraces all forms of mortal life and is forever renewing itself, while the blossoms symbolise the short span of man's life.

Ranking next to the chrysanthemum in its use in flower arrangement, but not in the esteem of the Japanese, comes the pine ; foremost of all evergreens it symbolises faithfulness, strength and endurance. Associated with the crane and the tortoise, both emblems of longevity, it expresses the idea of a long and hardy life. This combination is found in all the arts, but especially in pictorial art. For the celebration of a wedding a miniature representation of this grouping is indispensable ; often the figures of an old man and woman are added and it becomes known as the pine tree of "*Takasago.*" The old man and the old woman represent the spirits of two pine trees. *Takasago* is the name of a *Noh* or "Dance Drama" in which these trees are described and the chanting of this *Noh* is seldom neglected at a wedding. In this *Noh* the pine is considered emblematic of loyalty to the *Tenno*.

This combination of the pine with the crane and the tortoise is also used for the New Year holidays; though for a wedding a certain kind of pine must be used, the needles of which grow in pairs and when one withers and dies the other drops also, for New Year's decorations any kind may be used.

For a New Year's flower arrangement the pine is combined with the bamboo and the early plum blossom; this grouping is known as the *Sho chiku bai*. Like the pictorial crane and tortoise and pine, the *Sho chiku bai* arrangement is an essential part of a wedding or other happy occasion. The plum blossom is used as a symbol of chastity and is the emblem of the spirit of womanhood, as the cherry is of manhood, because, undaunted by the cold of winter, the plum sends forth its blossoms while the snow is yet on the ground. The bamboo typifies the virtue of straightforwardness; while here the pine is thought to suggest prosperity because its needles are always green and unchanging.

In art the bamboo is associated with the tiger and the sparrow, but never with both at the same time as are the crane and tortoise with the pine. A tiger pictured in a bamboo forest is said to be emblematic of safety because the elephant, natural enemy of the tiger, cannot penetrate such a jungle. The sparrow pictured with the bamboo is said to suggest the idea of loyalty to the throne, through association with old Chinese stories. From China also comes the story of the seven wise men who lived in a bamboo grove.

So closely are the various symbols connected in the Japanese mind that it would be unthinkable for them to display a painting of a tiger and an arrangement of common garden flowers at the same time. As an accompaniment of a pictured tiger some form of bamboo must be used for the flower arrangement.

The cherry blossom, rivalling the chrysanthemum in the affections of the Japanese, does not play so great a part in flower arrangement. It is never used in combination with anything except pine and must always have the place of honour in the room. No other flowers may be displayed in its presence.

In literature and especially in the hearts of the Japanese people the cherry blossom is associated with the training of the *samurai*. While the pine is used to symbolise the virtues of unswerving loyalty and faithfulness and for that is prized by the *samurai*, the cherry symbolises a more innately Japanese conception of the relation of the individual to the group. For the cherry is to them the model of all knightly conduct and knightly conduct has been the standard striven for by all classes. Individually the cherry blossom possesses no great charm ; it lacks the sweet scent of the plum and has no particular beauty of form, but in a mass on the tree it is a thing of almost unreal beauty. Its habit of bursting into sudden bloom to entrance its admirers for the short space of three or four days only to disappear as suddenly as it blooms prefigures to the Japanese the duty of every *samurai* to put forth his best efforts loyally and cheerfully and to die gladly without lingering, when his duty is accomplished. As the single cherry blossom is insignificant in itself, but as part of a tree an important unit in a thing of beauty, so the individual Japanese counts himself as nothing except as a part of his country's glory.

A peculiarity of the Japanese cherry is strangely like a peculiarity of the Japanese nature. There is a large element of inconsistency in the development and growth of these trees. In individual trees of the same species one finds variation in colour of foliage, size of flowers and even in the shape of the petals. The Japanese, despite a superficial appearance to the contrary, are the most individualistic of all peoples, in the sense that while seeking to be a harmonious part of the whole social body they seem to be constitutionally unable to lose their own individuality and to produce a thing exactly like their neighbours, or even two of the same thing exactly alike. It is well known that only on dress parades are the Japanese soldiers forced to walk in step ; the effort to do so is too tiring ; on long marches each goes his own gait.

The cherry, the symbol of service and sacrifice, is the symbol of the spirit of the Japanese people but there is no hint of sadness in this spirit; it is one of joy and gladness as is attested by the gay holiday crowds that throng the places famous for the beauty of these blossoms. Europeans sometimes deplore the fact that with all the blossoms the Japanese have no cherries but the Japanese scorn the idea and actually feel sorry for the peoples whose cherry blossoms are put to such mundane ends. Cherry blossom are for beauty and joy and symbolism, not for use.

A purely Japanese association of ideas is that of the small green tree-frog with the willow, because of the story of Ono-no-Dofu. Ono-no-Dofu was a Japanese nobleman of the tenth century who reached the ripe age of sixty without attaining proficiency in callig-raphy, that so admired art of writing the beautiful but difficult Chinese characters. One day as he was strolling beside the river, discouraged at his efforts towards this accomplishment, he noticed a tiny frog trying to reach a leaf on a hanging branch of willow. The frog tried again and again and on the seventh attempt succeeded in reaching his goal. The perseverance of this tiny creature so impressed Ono-no-Dofu that he returned home

78

determined not to be less courageous than so lowly a creature and applied himself with renewed vigour to his studies, with the result that he became one of the greatest calligraphers of his time.

Pendant branches of willow with a frog on the ground beneath are often used as design for lacquered writing desks and even as wood carvings for a room intended to be used as a study. Because the willow is a water-loving tree it is often arranged to suggest a pond-side scene in floral compositions, and a small bronze frog is placed in an inconspicuous corner of the container. The willow is called " weeping willow " by the Europeans, but it suggests no such connotation to the Japanese mind ; rather it suggests growth and fresh new life. A formal arrangement of willow branches and red camellia blossoms symbolises to them a young girl clad in gay garments.

Omoto—to the Western mind this plant is uninteresting and not quite suitable material for a flower arrangement, but the Japanese are very fond of it and use it for all happy occasions. Its sturdy glossy green leaves retain their colour the year round and its berries, which turn red in Winter, make a refreshing bit of colour for the holiday season. Because its name is written with characters which can also be read " ten thousand years green " it is a favourite arrangement for the celebration of the inauguration of any undertaking ; it is the accepted arrangement for any house-warming or wedding ; the first arrangement that the bride makes in her new home. An arrangement of these leaves will retain its freshness for weeks.

For the proper observance of any festival an appropriate flower arrangement is necessary and an arrangement's appropriateness is determined either by symbolism or literary allusion ; the flowers used are those naturally available at the season of the year in which the festival occurs.

Mention has already been made of the *Sho chiku bai,* Pine-Plum-Bamboo combination, and the *Shi kunshi* or Four Cultured Gentlemen combination of pine, bamboo, chrysanthemum and orchid, but for New Year flower arrangements certain other plants are also considered desirable because of their symbolic meaning and to add colour to the composition. *Yuzuriha* is the name of the small low-growing shrub with glossy green leaves and bright red berries which is used for its suggestion of a happy family because the old leaves of this plant do not drop off till the new ones have reached perfection, prefiguring the continued well-being of the father till the son is old enough to assume charge of the family. A small yellow blossom similar to the European crocus is used because the sound of the name *"fukuju so"* resembles the word for good fortune and because it pushes its way up through the snow and appears even before the plum blossom, symbolising the fertility of life hidden in the ground. The narcissus or Chinese lily is also used at this season ; called the child of two seasons because it blossoms just as winter merges into spring, it signifies strength, courage and purity.

For the Festival of Dolls, or *Ohina-sama* which occurs on the third day of the third month, both the cherry and the peach blossom are called into use. Originally Japanese festivals were reckoned by the Lunar Calendar and were celebrated a month later when these flowers were in natural bloom ; now they must be forced in hothouses or procured from warmer places. The cherry is represented by an artificial tree placed at one side before the two chief dolls but the peach blossom is used in its real form arranged in an informal arrangement with a few sprays of yellow wild mustard blossom (*nano hana*). The peach blossom is probably used because of the associated idea of the peach as the symbol of life.

The celebration of the Boys' Festival, or *Tango no sekku* on the fifth day of the fifth month, coincides with the blossoming of a form of iris, *shobu no hana.* The sound of its name " *shobu* " means also military valour and the shape of its leaves suggests a sword. An iris arrangement is displayed in all homes on this day.

On the seventh day of the seventh month the festival of *Tanabata*, a star festival, is celebrated. On that day entire bamboo trees hung with long narrow slips of coloured paper are displayed outside every door. Scarcely to be listed as a flower arrangement, this decoration is a very frequently seen art motif.

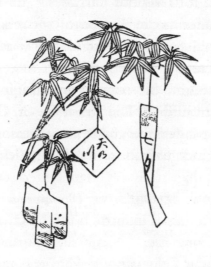

The association of the wild bush-clover, *hagi*, with the full moon of the eighth month is of literary origin, and this combination is a great favourite for decorated lacquer ware.

The Seven Flowers of Autumn include both flowers and grasses and the exact composition of this grouping is not known, some authorities naming flowers that others ignore. In art any of these plants, either alone or in combination, may be found associated with various field insects; and a flower arrangement of one or more is considered necessary for the ceremonial viewing of the moon.

Flowers of poisonous nature or of evil odour are never used for flower arrangement, and there are some that are used but sparingly. Those that change colour or fade, such as maple, wistaria, hydrangea and some others, are avoided on occasions of any importance because of their suggestion of changeableness.

Arrangements of lotus are sometimes made in the middle of summer because it is the season's blossom but orthodox Buddhists avoid its use except for religious purposes. It is considered suitable for funeral decorations because of its religious associations. When used for mid-summer arrangements it is combined with reeds or marsh grasses. When arranged alone it is a symbol of human life suggesting past, present and future. Large perfect green leaves and full-blown blossoms represent the present ; dried and broken leaves and seed-pods represent the past ; while the future is suggested by buds of both flower and leaf. In pictorial art and sculpture the Buddha is always represented seated on a lotus blossom.

There is a division of thought regarding roses, a modern importation but one which takes kindly to this soil and flourishes. The most important objection is that as yet no method of keeping them fresh and unwilted has been discovered, and moreover flowers with thorns have never been popular for flower arrangement. However some schools delight in arranging them with pine branches for the contrast of their colour and form against the sturdy green.

Stones are sometimes used to complete a floral composition. For iris or water-growing plants small pebbles are best, but to simulate the edge of a lake large water-worn stones are often used. Occasionally, especially in the hot weather, a large irregular-shaped stone, vaguely suggestive of a mountain, is used as the main part of the arrangement and small water plants are arranged at its base in a shallow container. In that case the whole arrangement is kept dripping wet.

Stones are also used alone, arranged according to the rules of *Ike-bana*, for their suggestion of strength and coolness.

SECRETS OF JAPANESE FLOWER
ARRANGEMENT

THE spirit of a Japanese flower arrangement is to make a thing of beauty out of commonplace materials. No shrub is too rugged nor flower too humble to be used for this purpose. It may be somewhat startling to our readers for us to assert that the West can learn efficiency from the East—but such is the case with flower arrangement. With the Japanese method far fewer flowers are used to obtain a given effect. Not only is the colour of the flower considered, but its leaves and its general shape

as well.   Each flower is placed so as to show to the best advantage.
Given any flower with its accompanying leaves, the Japanese method
will make a more interesting and pleasing arrangement of five
blossoms than the European method (or lack of method) can with
a dozen.

There is a wealth of material for flower arrangements in any
garden, overlooked by those obsessed with the idea that only a
mass of full-blown blossoms will suffice for a floral piece.   In
Spring the tender green leaf buds, in Autumn the sere seed-pods
can be used to good advantage combined with blossoms for colour
contrast.

The convention of leaving half or more than half of the
container free from flowers showing the water produces a sense of
restfulness often sadly lacking in a crowded bouquet.

A WORD TO THOSE WHO INTEND TO MAKE
A STUDY OF FLOWER ARRANGEMENT

While the formal *Ike-no-bo* arrangements are not suitable for
all houses, a little time spent on mastering the rules governing
their construction will more than repay the flower lover in acquir-
ing confidence and speed in making the more informal arrangements.   As is explained elsewhere in this book, the basic principles
of *Ike-no-bo* are art principles ; any arrangement of flowers, whether
of a single rose and its leaves or great branches for hall or church
decoration, will be more quickly arranged and produce more
aesthetic pleasure if due regard is paid to these principles.

The Japanese dislike the word triangle applied to their flower
arrangements ; they prefer the more aesthetic term " crescent-moon-

shaped," but the western mind more readily grasps the idea of a triangle. An *Ike-no-bo* arrangement is triangular in shape made of three smaller triangular-shaped groups of branches; if this is kept in mind in making a *Nageire* or *Moribana* arrangement, the desired results are obtained easily and quickly.

There are times when one branch will make a perfect arrangement; sometimes many are necessary. Care should be taken to use an odd number of branches, flowers or fruits, never an even number. Keep the composition sparse; do not crowd. Always leave at least half the opening of the container free from flowers. Flowers arranged in this loose manner keep longer than when crowded into the mouth of a container. When a basket with a handle is used see that the handle is left clear so that the basket may be carried.

In measuring height of branches allowance must be made for depth of container. Slender weak tips are not considered, only the strongest part of the branch is measured. Although rules are given for determining the lengths of the principal branches, judgment must be used. Necessarily these rules are flexible; all flowers are different and each requires a different treatment.

The fundamental rules for a Japanese flower arrangement are :—

FIRST.   Correct proportion between flowers and container and place of display is essential.

SECOND.   An arrangement must express natural growth and stems of flowers must leave the mouth of the container as a growing unit.

THIRD.   Never have two branches or flowers of the same height.

FOURTH. Do not use too many flowers ; allow each to be seen
from its base up.

The authors of this book urge any student of flower arrangement to study and memorise the general shape of *Ike-no-bo*
arrangements, especially the proportions of the arrangement to its
container, and of the branches making up the three main groups.

Every Japanese flower arrangement is made up of these three
groups of plant material, always occupying the same relative
positions.

For convenience of explanation we have retained the use of
the Japanese terms *Shin, Soe, Tai.*

Shin is the tallest and main central group.

Soe is the intermediate, or harmonising group.

Tai is the shortest group.

These terms have been sanctioned by centuries of use here in

Shin Branch

Japan and, because of their implied meanings,
are more aesthetically correct than any merely
mechanical designations.   For a detailed explanation of these terms see chapter on *Ike-no-bo.*

SHIN GROUP :—This group determines
the size of the arrangement ; all other groups
are in fixed proportions to it and are grouped
about it.   The tip of the main *Shin* branch
should be directly over the point of that
branch's emergence from the container, regardless of the general shape of the branch.   This
Shin branch is the central point or pivot of
the entire arrangement ; in making an arrangement, branches or flowers in the rear of this
branch are considered as in the shade, or subject

90

to a northern exposure; those in front of this *Shin* branch are considered as in the sunshine, or as subject to a southern exposure. Therefore, as a rule, buds or weather-beaten plant materials are used in the rear of this branch and full-blown blossoms or new young shoots of plant material in front.

SOE GROUP :—This group should spread fanwise with tips of branches or flowers having an upward bend, as though growing toward the *Shin* group. It is most important that the stem of the main *Soe* branch be easily distinguishable—it should never have twigs, branches or flowers drooping lifelessly on its underside. To avoid this, cut off any that cannot be bent to follow the line of the main stem.

Soe Branch

TAI or NEJIME :—In any arrangement of any style the main *Tai* branch must turn upwards at the tip as though growing to-

wards the tip of *Shin* and it must not have small branches, twigs or flowers extending downward from it; those that cannot be bent or coaxed to follow the line of the main stem must be cut off.

Both the *Soe* and *Tai* branches might be termed the frame of their respective groups, because flowers are never added beyond their stem lines; always add flowers between those branches and the main branch.

Tai Branch

The modern handcraft pottery in odd and individual shapes is excellent for flower arrangement. Those with a soft dull glaze, rather than a hard brilliant one, tone in with the flowers and add to their beauty. Basket-shaped containers need few flowers; never fill them full, and always leave the handle unobstructed by the flowers, so that the basket may easily be lifted if necessary.

An interesting idea for table decoration, and one entirely in keeping with Japanese tradition, is a small neutral-coloured soft-glaze pottery container on a flat black or contrasting-coloured board (or stand) using one, two or three blossoms with their natural leaves. Discard the idea that a quantity of flowers is necessary, and give attention to selecting a background for a simple arrangement of a few flowers.

A single flower with its accompanying leaves taken from a potted plant and arranged in a container to show to the best advantage will often give more pleasure than the entire potted plant, especially if the flower and its container are placed on an odd-shaped board or stand. Unlike the Western method of arrangement, Japanese arrangement does not need special containers—the art lies in using common everyday articles to make a thing of beauty.

Covered dishes arranged with a very few flowers and with the cover itself as a part of the composition can be used to good advantage.

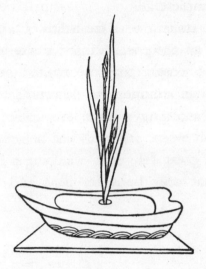

Clean water and fresh air are the best preservatives of any flower, and for this reason flowers arranged in the Japanese manner will far outlast those arranged in the usual Western manner of cramming them tightly into a small-mouthed vase. There is no chemical known that will take the place of careful handling and fresh clean water.

Every Japanese flower teacher has his own secret methods of preserving different flowers to be divulged only after years of study, but the following suggestions will be of help to flower lovers in any country :

In gathering and arranging flowers be careful not to crush the leaves. If time permits : any flower will last longer if immediately after cutting it is set aside for a few hours in a cool dark place submerged all but the blossoms in water. For delicate flowers, wrap each blossom separately in soft tissue paper before placing stems in water. In handling white or easily damaged flowers the Japanese keep the blossoms so wrapped until the arrangement is complete.

In Japan the making of a fresh flower arrangement is as indispensable a part of the preparation for guests as are the proper refreshments. To ensure that the invited guest will have the utmost pleasure in an arrangement, flowers that open quickly, such as certain lilies, morning glories, magnolias, cactuses, etc., are kept tied up in soft white paper till just before the guest's arrival. The Japanese take great delight in watching a flower unfold; it is for this reason that only buds are used and full-blown flowers avoided.

Branches of trees, evergreen or fruit-bearing, need no artificial preservative. With your pruning shears split the end of the branch for a couple of inches; if small enough the branch may be crushed by hammering; or if too large to cut, strip off most of the bark under the water.

A ten percent solution of hydrochloric acid is a good quick way of preserving flowers, but it cannot be recommended, as care must be taken in handling it—it will stain any material with which it comes in contact.

Simple household materials that can be used to advantage are :—dry sugar rubbed into the crushed ends of asters ; dry boric acid rubbed into carnation stems; and dry powdered aspirin tablets rubbed into the ends of dahlias and chrysanthemums.

A mixture of equal parts of dry salt and alum rubbed into the stems of poppies or dahlias will keep them from wilting—or they may be charred as you would chrysanthemums.

Common dry salt may be rubbed into the ends of columbine or the stems may be dipped into peppermint oil for a second.

Sugar water is recommended for all soft or hollow-stemmed flowers ; or they may be treated as follows :—cut end freshly and rub peppermint oil or menthol into the cut end with the finger. Do not dip into the acid because that softens and destroys the stems.

Use a small water pump or syringe to force water into hollow stemmed flowers such as water lilies, calla lilies, etc. A weak solution of tobacco juice is good for cowslips. Powdered alum rubbed into the stem ends of plants such as exude lactiferous juice is good.

Alcohol is recommended for wistaria—first char the ends of the branches then place them for some time in alcohol.

Break, do not cut, chrysanthemum or hydrangea.

A rusted pin stuck into the stem of a morning glory will prolong its beauty for many hours, or the end of the stem may be crushed and dry salt rubbed into it.

When gathering flowers that wilt easily it is a good idea to take with you a bottle containing a weak solution of sugar-water and to place the flowers in this as soon as cut.

Such woody and strong-stemmed plants as are listed below may be treated either by charring the ends or by placing them in boiling water. These flowers also may be revived and their beauty prolonged for several hours by hot water treatment:

*Aster.	*Hydrangea.
*Azalea.	Jews Mallow.
Bell flower.	Marigold.
Carnation.	*Red Berries.
*Chrysanthemum.	*Peony.

Dahlia.	Poppy.
Day Lily.	Rose.
*Ferns.	Spanish Broom.
Garden Pink.	Thistle.

* Marks those which respond best to charring.

TO CHAR.—Carefully wrap entire branch or flower in towel or newspaper to keep heat from leaves; expose only two or three inches and char in flame of any kind. Do not char more than half an inch of the stem. Unwrap and hold upside-down and pour clean cold water over the entire branch. Now take each branch separately and carefully arrange all leaves parallel with the stems; flowers straight on stems, not bent at an angle; wrap loosely in newspaper and set away for an hour. When doing this it is best to have blossoms wrapped in bits of soft paper.

HOT WATER TREATMENT.—Wrap the entire branch to keep steam from leaves and dip about one inch of the stems in boiling water for not more than two minutes. Then treat as above, or put in a deep container of cold water and spray leaves.

97

TO REVIVE MOST WOODY-STEMMED FLOWERS :—Sometimes in arranging such flowers as chrysanthemums the leaves become wilted and drooping. They can be freshened, as can also flowers that are past their first freshness. In case of an *Ike-no-bo* arrangement in the usual bronze container, merely pour off the old water ; or use tall narrow container of a kind that will stand boiling water. Carefully cover the mouth of the container so that the steam will not reach the leaves ; use a towel or newspaper. Pour in about two inches of boiling water and let stand till the water is cool. Spray the arrangement with cold water and straighten and encourage the leaves to reach upwards ; you can see the strength coming back into them. Fill the container with cold water after the hot water has cooled to room temperature.

TRADITIONAL STYLE

OF

JAPANESE
FLOWER ARRANGEMENT

IKE-NO-BO

THE purpose of this book is to encourage the beginner to further efforts to adapt the traditional Japanese method of flower arrangement to his own needs. With that idea in mind we have made a brief outline of the various types of *Ike-no-bo* arrangements in the order in which they are taught, beginning with the simplest and progressing to the more difficult. We have used the Japanese nomenclature for the different parts of the arrangement rather than the English for the reason that there is no adequate

101

translation for the terms *Shin, Soe, Tai,* etc. Each of these words conveys more meaning than any English word could and all English equivalents fall short. Japanese words are used also for the convenience of those who may study flower arrangement in Japan.

> *Ushiro* means " in the rear " ; with the word " *Soe* " this word is used first and " s " changes to " z ". *Soe-ushiro* (in back of *Soe*) is always pronounced *Ushirozoe. Shin-ushiro* means " in back of *Shin,*" *Tai-ushiro* means " in back of *Tai.*"

> *Mae* means " in front," and like *ushiro* when in combination with *Soe* takes first position. *Shin-mae* means " in front of *Shin* "; *Maezoe* means " in front of *Soe.*"

The use of these terms has persisted for centuries here in Japan and to the student who finds them confusing we suggest that he or she number the groups. The use of numbers in sample lessons is impossible for no two arrangements are ever exactly the same. Our aim is to set forth the basic principles underlying all arrangements ; so that the student may use her own materials and not be tempted to confine herself to the materials used in the sample lesson.

The Japanese method of arranging flowers known as the *Ike-no-bo* school of arrangement has been practised for centuries and years of study are necessary to master it. But even a slight and superficial knowledge of it is a help in the more simple forms of arrangement and will prove of great value to any lover of flowers. Alfred Kohen, in his comprehensive book entitled, " The Way of Japanese Flower Arrangement," has gone into this subject exhaustively, and his book is recommended to those who wish to investigate further this fascinating subject.

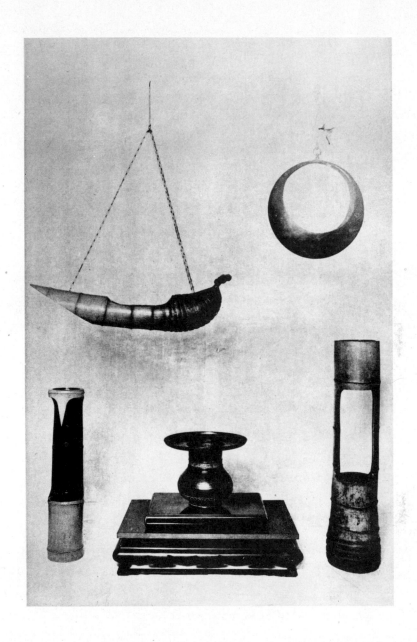

Types of containers commonly used for Ike-no-bo arrangements.

An *Ike-no-bo* arrangement is unsuitable for any but certain traditional containers. These are bronze vases of various designs, called *Usubata*, whose distinguishing feature is a plate-like top. If an *Usubata* is not obtainable, use a bronze vase, about twelve to fifteen inches high. For practice the Japanese use a simple bamboo tube-like vase about fifteen inches high.

An *Ike-no-bo* arrangement may be made of three branches only, or of thirty-three. There are always the three groups of *Shin, Soe, Tai*. These groups may contain only one branch or many. However for the best results each group will again be made with three points similar to *Shin, Soe, Tai*, complete in itself but conforming to the whole.

Any *Ike-no-bo* arrangement is a development of these three groups. The number of branches or flowers necessary depends on the plant material used. An odd number of branches is used in each group, as well as in the arrangement as a whole. The difference in lengths of branches should be the same throughout the whole arrangement. Proportion is an essential requirement in any flower arrangement. Cut the branch in the rear of the main branch first—the branch or branches in front of the main branch (such as *Shin, Soe, Tai*) should be shorter than those that are behind. Always make the branch in the rear of any group main branch longer than the one in front of the main branch.

In arranging consider yourself as the sun and insert flowers as though naturally turning to the sun. As a rule, buds should be used for the tips of the main branches; full-blown flowers are used for the centre and lower part of the arrangement. Be sure that all tips point upwards, whatever the curve of the branch. Do not allow any downward reaching branches in the *Soe* group. The arrangement must leave the surface of the water as a single unit; do not allow any leaves to droop downwards.

Ike-no-bo arrangements may be either right or left handed— the direction in which the *Tai* branch points determines the name. A *Hongatte* or right-hand arrangement should be placed on the left of the table or shelf, with the *Tai* branch pointing towards the centre of the table or stand on which it is placed ; it should never point into space aimlessly.

Do not be afraid to cut flowers and branches to the desired shape.   In the last analysis it is beauty you are endeavouring to express and if that end is served by the sacrifice of blossoms or twigs, beautiful in themselves but unnecessary for your purpose, do not hesitate to destroy them.   Remember mere oddness is not beauty ; poverty of material is not desirable—there is a difference between restraint and paucity of material—but the Japanese idea is to eliminate all material that does not directly contribute to the beauty of the finished composition.   However, profusion is not a synonym for beauty in any flower arrangement.

In the diagrams a complete group of branches or flowers is indicated by three lines, and with the exception of the three longest lines, the *Shin* branch, the *Soe* branch and the *Tai* branch, each line may be made up of more than one branch ; or the arrangement may be made of the main branches only.   Measurements are figured from the mouth of the container, and only the sturdy growth is measured.

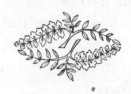

HOW TO CUT AND SHAPE FLOWERING
TREE BRANCHES

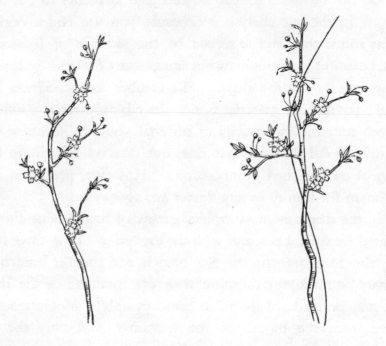

SHIN GROUP

Select a long straight branch and bend to conform with usual curve of the *Ike-no-bo Shin* branch.   Cut off all small twigs and leaves that obscure the line of the main branch.   Sometimes attached branches can be used for *Shin-ushiro* and *Shin-mae* ; if not, select other branches and trim and bend to shape.   The blossoms of this group face the arranger.

SOE GROUP

Sometimes a branch can be found whose curve approximates the *Soe* curve of the *Ike-no-bo* arrangement; if not, trim and bend one to the desired shape. For *Ushirozoe* and *Maezoe* select suitable branches; trim and bend into desired shape. The blossoms of this group face the *Shin* group of the arrangement and no blossoms or small twigs should be allowed to droop downwards.

109

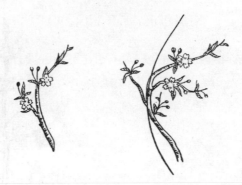

TAI GROUP

If possible select a branch whose curve approximates the curve of the *Ike-no-bo Tai* branch ; or cut and bend one into that shape. The blossoms of this group should face the *Shin* group and none should be allowed to droop downwards.

110

SIMPLE IKE-NO-BO

A formal arrangement of flowering tree branches, grasses or long-stemmed flowers, arranged in a bamboo tube-like container, or bronze *Usubata*, traditional vase for these arrangements; any bronze vase may be substituted.

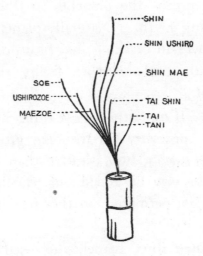

General Instructions for *Ike-no-bo* Arrangement.
Using Any Tree Branch or Long-Stemmed Flowers.

SHIN GROUP

Shin.—Select a long slender branch with a strong tip : or if using flowers, a bud if possible. Cut the main branch equal to $2^{1}/_{2}$ times the height of the container, plus the depth of the container ; because all branches must rest firmly on the bottom of the container.

Shin-ushiro.—Cut a little shorter than *Shin*; be careful to

111

keep the branch in the rear of the *Shin* branch thin and scant, not full blossomed. If using flowers select tight buds or small blossoms.

Shin-mae.—Cut a little shorter than *Shin-ushiro* ; use full-flowered branch or half-opened flower.

The rear of the *Shin* is supposed to represent the north—the branches in front of the *Shin* are facing south. Naturally plants to the north are slower in breaking into blossom than those in the south, and branches facing the south blossom best.

If more than these three branches or flowers are necessary in the *Shin* group, add a second *Shin-mae*, a little shorter than the first *Shin-mae*. A second *Shin-ushiro* may be added but usually one branch or flower is all that is permitted in the rear of the main *Shin* branch.

When more than three branches are used a taller *Shin-ushiro* is necessary—the difference in height of any two adjacent branches must be the same throughout the entire arrangement.

In working with flowers, keep buds towards the tips of the groups, and full-blown flowers for the centre of the arrangement.

The branch behind *Shin* (*Shin-ushiro*) is often imperfect ; never use a perfect full-blown blossom here.

SOE GROUP

This group branches out in the opposite direction to the *Shin* and *Tai* groups. The *Ushirozoe*, rear branch, and the *Maezoe*,

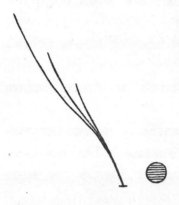

front branch, are really on top of the main *Soe* branch rather than in front of it and behind it, though the tips spread fanwise, and the shortest comes more to the front than the other two.

Cut main branch ⅔ the length of the *Shin* branch. Add one branch or more. Be careful that no small branches or leaves extend downwards from this group. If using flowers select bud for the *Soe* branch, half-open flower for the *Ushirozoe*, blossom for *Maezoe*.

If more than three blossoms or branches are necessary, add a second *Ushirozoe*—then a second *Maezoe*. Keep in mind that the increase in the number of branches or flowers diminishes the difference in length of any two adjacent branches or flowers. See that the tips of all branches or flowers turn up slightly as if to catch and hold the dew.

TAI GROUP

This branch points forward and seems to be reaching out to the viewer. All blossoms must be kept on top of the branch.

Cut *Tai* branch ⅓ the length of the *Shin* branch. Cut the tallest branch, or *Tai Shin*, ½ the length of the *Shin* branch of the *Shin* group. Actually the *Tai* branch of the *Tai* group is often the same height as the *Tai Shin* because, being nearer the viewer, it is foreshortened.

The Japanese word *Tani* means "valley," and the *Tani* branch or group is the lowest part of any Japanese flower arrangement.

If more than three flowers or branches are necessary in the *Tai* group, add in the following sequence :—

FIRST.   *Tai Shin-ushiro*—branch or flower behind the *Tai Shin*.

SECOND.   *Tai Shin-mae*—branch or flower before the *Tai Shin*.

THIRD.   Two or more branches or flowers between *Tai Shin* and *Shin-mae*. Do not have any two branches or flowers the same height.

If using flowers for the *Tai* group, all except the *Tai* branch itself may be full-blown blossoms ; the *Tai* branch should have a bud at the tip if possible. Trim off most of the leaves on the under side of the branch and never allow a downward drooping leaf or twig. The tip must turn upward as if growing.

TO SHAPE

SHIN GROUP

Stand main *Shin* branch upright in container. Consider carefully and turn the best side towards yourself. Every branch or flower has one side better than the other—the side that has been growing towards the sun—that side must face you. Now, at a point just below half-way between the mouth of the container and the tip of this branch, gently bend it, to the right for a right-hand arrangement, *Hongatte*, and to the left for a left-hand arrangement, *Gyakugatte*. At $^2/_3$ of the distance between this bend and the tip gently bend it the other way. You should now have a softly curved branch with the tip directly in a line

114

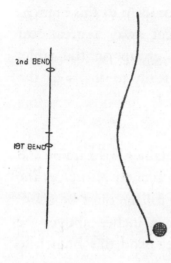

with the base. Exercise the utmost care with this branch, as its shape decides the shape of the entire arrangement.

Now make all the other branches or flowers of this group conform to this branch.

Do not attempt to bend plant material which naturally grows straight, but any soft pliant material may be quite definitely curved.

Lay this *Shin* group down by itself —it is now ready to place in the container.

SOE GROUP

Stand the main *Soe* branch in the container. Examine carefully—the best side of this branch should be faced upwards. In this case the *Shin* branch may be considered as the sun with the leaves turning naturally that way. Now, at a point about 5 inches

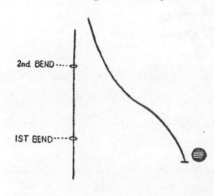

above the mouth of the container, bend this branch; to the left for a right-hand arrangement, and to the right for a left-hand arrangement. The curve of this branch is away from the *Shin* branch, though it clings closely to this branch up to the bending point. Again, at a

point ²/₃ of the way between this bend and the tip of the branch, bend it back the other way. The tip of this branch should point upwards and towards the *Shin* branch.

Bend all other branches or flowers to conform to this branch. With some plant material it is necessary to cut away a great deal of the foliage of this group. Lay the *Soe* group on the table, separate from the *Shin* group. It is now ready to insert in the container.

TAI GROUP

Stand the *Tai* branch upright in the container. Examine and determine the best side of the foliage. This branch also faces the *Shin* branch—on the outside or underside the foliage must be scant.

2ND BEND

1ST BEND

At a point about two inches above the mouth of the container bend this branch to the right for a right-hand arrangement, or to the left for a left-hand arrangement. Now, $^2/_3$ of the way between this bend and the tip of the branch, bend it back so that the tip appears to be growing ; do not allow it to droop as if dead.

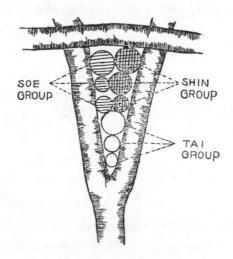

SOE GROUP

SHIN GROUP

TAI GROUP

Showing position of branch groups in *kubari* with *komi* in place.

116

The *kubari* is a forked stick inserted in the mouth of the container, about $1/2$ an inch below the surface of the water, into which the flowers or branches are forced and so held upright.

Any naturally forked branch may be used, or a tough branch may be split and forced open to form a " Y " shaped holder. A short strong piece of plant material termed *komi* is used to clamp the arrangement into place in the *kubari*.

Place your vase firmly on the table in front of you; do not turn it as you work, and always stand directly in front of it. Turn the *kubari* (or forked stick to hold the flowers upright) point toward you.

Bear in mind that while only one *ushiro* or *mae* branch is called for in this explanation, it may be necessary to have several *ushiro* or several *mae* branches—the number is determined by the plant material you are working with.

There can be only one main branch in each of the three groups, but any number of auxiliary ones.

FIRST STEP

TAI GROUP.—Take up the *Tai*[1] branch from the *Tai* group. Place it firmly in the holder, resting on the bottom of the container, and with the left hand hold it firmly in place, upright, as far in the angle of the *kubari* as you can force it. Insert the remaining branches of the *Tai* group, forcing them in tightly behind the *Tai* branch along the right fork of the *kubari* in the following order :—*Tai Tani*,[2] *Tai Shin*.[3]

117

SECOND STEP

SHIN GROUP.—Holding the *Tai* group firmly in place, take up *Shin-mae*[4] and insert it behind the *Tai* branches. Next insert the *Shin*[5] branch, keeping all the branches in place with your left hand. Next insert the *Shin-ushiro*.[6] The branches should be in this order in the *kubari*, well over against the right arm of the fork. Remember that both *Shin-mae* and *Shin-ushiro* may consist of several branches or flowers.

THIRD STEP

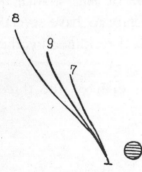

SOE GROUP.—Lastly take up the *Maezoe*[7] branch and insert it well towards the front of the *kubari* and at the left side of the *Shin* group of branches. After the *Maezoe* branch insert the *Soe*,[8] then the *Ushirozoe*[9] branch. *Maezoe* and *Ushirozoe* may consist of several branches or flowers. These branches are forced between the *Shin* group branches and the left arm of the *kubari*.

FOURTH STEP

Now cut a straight piece of plant material, same as that forming the *kubari* is excellent, and force it into place behind the stems of the arrangement to hold them firmly in place. Sometimes it is necessary to insert one or more stems long enough to rest on the bottom of the container and engage the *komi* or fastening piece, but keep them as short as possible; they

118

must not be conspicuous. The *komi* must be straight; do not allow it to curve.

At this stage do not be concerned about the shape of the branches. See that all branches rest firmly on the bottom of the container, and that they are in alignment for about five inches above, as well as below, the mouth of the container. See that the tip of the *Shin* branch is over its base.

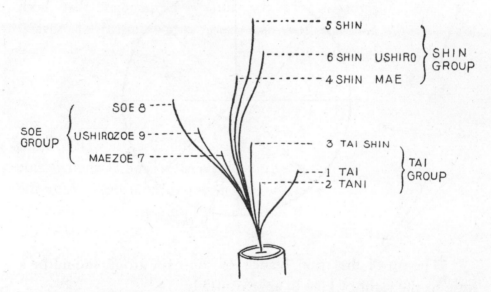

Do not hesitate to trim off all crossing and confusing small branches and leaves—the stem line of the three main branches should be easily recognised—bend and coax all small leaves and twigs to follow the line of the main stem. Give special attention to the *Soe* and *Tai* groups. Do not allow any downward-reaching leaves or twigs on the underside of either of these two branches. If possible bend flowers or twigs upwards—if not, cut them off.

The tips of all branches should be separated from the main branch just enough to be seen ; but the stems should leave the

119

surface of the water as one unit, like the trunk of a tree. The tips of the three main branches form a triangle, but in a good arrangement an imaginary line drawn close to the branches would he crescent shaped, not straight.

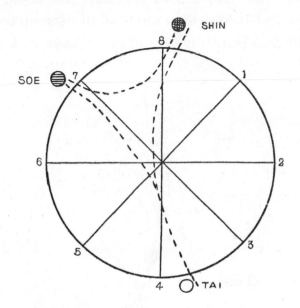

The tip of the main branch of the *Shin* group should be a little to the right of Line 8, approximately.

The tip of the main branch of the *Soe* group should extend a little to the left of Line 7, approximately.

The tip of the main branch of the *Tai* group should extend between Lines 3 and 4, nearest Line 4.

You can now attend to the final adjustments of the arrangement. Gently bend and coax branches into the desired shape. See that the tip of the *Shin* branch is over the stem of the arrangement where it emerges from the water. The tips of all the branches must bend upward the least bit, and flowers must face upwards. When finished, the arrangement should suggest a living plant—not a collection of branches.

IKE-NO-BO WITH NEJIME

An arrangement with a group of blossoms (*Nejime*) replacing the *Tai* group in the simple *Ike-no-bo*. *Nejime* is used only when there are no flowers in the *Shin* and *Soe* groups.

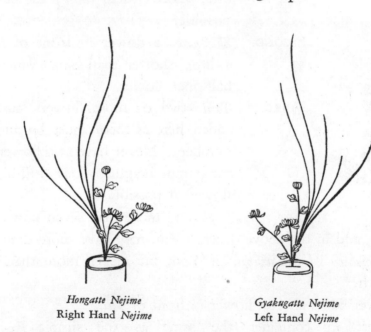

Hongatte Nejime
Right Hand *Nejime*

Gyakugatte Nejime
Left Hand *Nejime*

This group is made up of three or more flowers, depending on the size. Three large blossoms with accompanying leaves will be enough; but if small blossoms are used, seven, nine or even more will be necessary.

Cut *Tai Shin* half the length of the main *Shin* branch.

Cut the *Tai* flower, allowing for curve, so that the finished apparent height is $1/3$ the height of the main *Shin* branch. Actually

121

it is often the same length as the *Tai* branch (half the height of the main *Shin* branch); being directly in front of the viewer it appears foreshortened.

Cut the third flower of this group—*Tani*—at a height harmonious with the other two.

If more than three flowers are used, add :—

FIRST. *Shin-ushiro*—a flower behind *Shin*, a little shorter than *Shin* ; use bud if possible.

SECOND. *Shin-mae*—a flower in front of *Shin*, a little shorter than *Shin-ushiro*; use half-open flower.

THIRD. *Tani*—two or more flowers must be added here as there must be an odd number. Never have two flowers of the same height. Use full-blown flowers if possible.

Should more than seven flowers be necessary, add in the above order. You may have more than one *Tai Shin-ushiro* or *Tai-ushiro*, or *Tani*, but never more than one *Tai* branch.

Never add a shorter flower in front of *Tai*.

Insert in container the same as the simple *Ike-no-bo* arrangement.

NI-JU NO IKE-NO-BO

A double arrangement of *Ike-no-bo* made in a bamboo container. This style is not suitable for any other type of container. Tree or bush branches should be used for the upper arrangement, while flowers are required for the lower one; or two or more different flowers may be used. There are two types, either of which can be arranged either to the left or to the right.

The beauty of this arrangement depends on keeping the *Shin-Soe-Tai* groups of the upper arrangement as a single unit for some distance above the mouth of the container. Note the continuation of the line of *Shin* in both arrangements. You may have a *Nejime* with either of these arrangements.

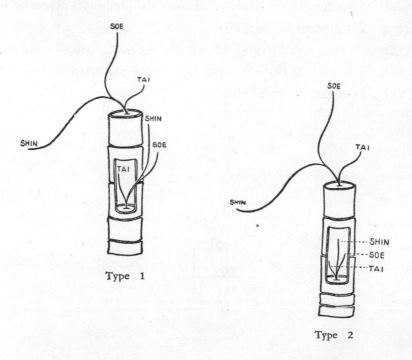

Type 1

Type 2

123

TO ARRANGE UPPER GROUP OF TYPE 1 OR TYPE 2

SHIN GROUP

For this style of arrangement, the *Shin* and *Soe* branches of the upper arrangement change places.

Cut *Shin* equal to the total length of the container. Bend into true *Soe* shape, and treat as the *Soe* group of simple *Ike-no-bo*.

SOE GROUP

Cut ⅔ the length of *Shin*, bend into *Shin* shape, and treat as the *Shin* group of the simple *Ike-no-bo*.

TAI GROUP

Cut ⅓ the length of *Shin*, bend into *Tai* shape and treat as the *Tai* group of the simple *Ike-no-bo*.

Insert in *kubari* according to simple *Ike-no-bo* rules. Keep in mind that each line of the diagram represents a group of branches or flowers, not just one branch.

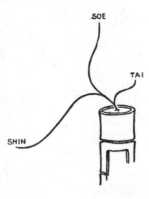

LOWER ARRANGEMENT, Type 1

Unless quite small, five to seven flowers are enough. Keep this arrangement scant, not full.

SHIN GROUP

Cut *Shin* so that tip just reaches the top of the container. If wished, add *Shin-ushiro* and *Shin-mae*.

SOE GROUP

Cut *Soe* branch ²/₃ of *Shin*. Add *Ushirozoe* and *Maezoe*, keep scant.

TAI GROUP

Cut *Tai* ¹/₃ of *Shin*. Add *Tani* if needed.

This arrangement should be the reverse of the upper one. The line of the *Soe* branch of the upper should appear to be a continuation of the *Shin* branch of the lower arrangement, a beautiful double curve.

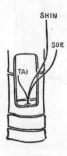

LOWER ARRANGEMENT, Type 2

SHIN GROUP

Cut length so that the tip of the *Shin* branch is just within the opening.   Add *Shin-ushiro* and *Shin-mae* if wished.

SOE GROUP

Cut ²/₃ the length of *Shin*.   Add *Ushirozoe* and *Maezoe* if needed.

TAI GROUP

Cut *Tai* ¹/₃ of *Shin*.   Add *Tani* if needed.

Note that the top of *Shin* in the lower arrangement is directly underneath the base of the *Shin* of the upper arrangement.   The lower arrangement is always scant, never full.   The upper arrangement is always the same regardless of the lower.

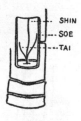

TACHI-NO-BORI

A simple yet difficult arrangement of branches or flowers in a bamboo container of conventional shape.

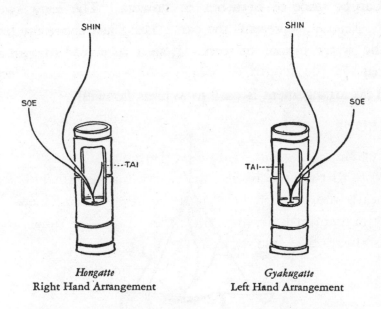

Hongatte
Right Hand Arrangement

Gyakugatte
Left Hand Arrangement

Cut *Shin* $1^{1}/_{2}$ times the height of the container, plus depth of same and arrange according to simple *Ike-no-bo*. Keep arrangement scant to show line of stems.

Do not allow any part of the arrangement to touch the container. The *Tai* branch should extend directly forward, so that the arrangement does not appear crowded into the container; almost half of the container opening should be clear of plant material, to produce a sense of restfulness.

127

DE-FUNE

or

Outgoing-Boat Arrangement.

Can be made of branches or flowers. The long sweeping branch, *Nagashi*, represents the oar. Hang just above eye level, so that the water cannot be seen. If seen it would suggest a leaking boat.

This arrangement is used to express farewell.

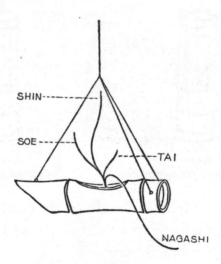

Follow the usual proportions for simple *Ike-no-bo*, keeping the tip of the *Shin* within the triangle formed by the supporting chains. Use as long a *Nagashi* as material will allow. *Nagashi* sweeps to the right.

Vines or drooping plant materials are best for this arrangement. The tips of *Shin*, *Soe* and *Tai* must be within the triangle formed by the supporting chains by which the boat is suspended.

IRI-FUNE

or

Incoming-Boat Arrangement.

The reverse of *De-fune*.   Expresses the wish for the return of a friend.   *Nagashi* should sweep to the left.

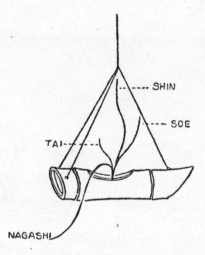

Follow the usual proportions for simple *Ike-no-bo*, keeping the tip of *Shin* within the triangle formed by the supporting chains. Use as long a *Nagashi* as material will allow.

TOMARI-FUNE

or

Standing-Boat Arrangement.

Expresses peace. Plant material of rather straight nature is preferred for this, usually irises or reeds.

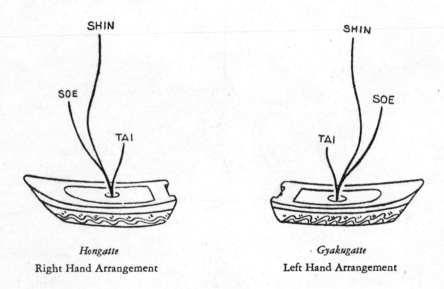

Hongatte
Right Hand Arrangement

Gyakugatte
Left Hand Arrangement

Cut *Shin* about the length of the boat. Do not bend. Follow the usual proportions for the simple *Ike-no-bo*.

TSUKI NO IKE-NO-BO

or

Arrangement in Moon-Shaped Container.

Sometimes flowers are used, but the arrangement is apt to be too stiff.   Vines or drooping plant materials are best.

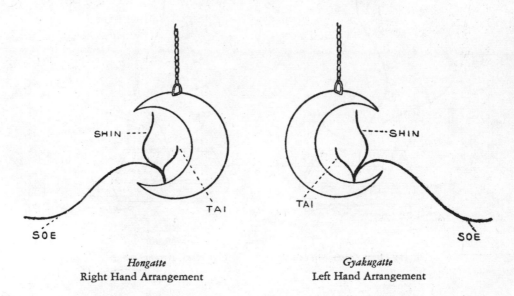

Hongatte
Right Hand Arrangement

Gyakugatte
Left Hand Arrangement

Follow instructions for simple *Ike-no-bo*.   Keep *Shin* well within the circumference of the crescent.

SUNABACHI

A development of simple *Ike-no-bo* in a large bronze container.

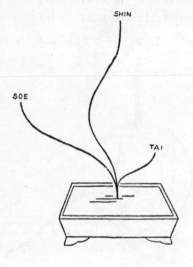

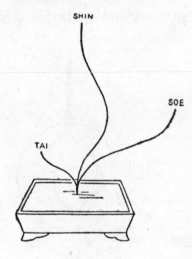

Hongatte
Right Hand Arrangement

Gyakugatte
Left Hand Arrangement

KAKE-HANA

or

Hanging Flower Arrangement.

A simple arrangement of any drooping plant material much like a *Nageire* arrangement.   This should be hung at a height so that the centre part of the arrangement is on a level with your eyes.

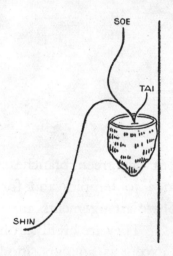

Hongatte
Right Hand Arrangement

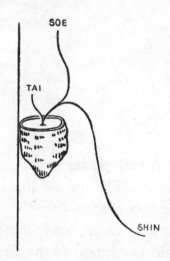

Gyakugatte
Left Hand Arrangement

133

RIKKA

A very ornate large arrangement of evergreen branches and flowers. The use of *Rikka* is confined to temples and formal decoration for the Imperial Court. These arrangements are very difficult to make, sometimes taking days. They are highly artificial and do not appeal to the flower lover, except as an exposition of skill in arrangement. However, in their proper setting, they are dignified and beautiful.

IKE-NO-BO

Hongatte or Right Hand Arrangement.

Willow and red camellia in basket. The willow naturally grows tall so cut *Shin* at least three times the height of the basket. Proportionally, the *Nejime* will be shorter—only about ¼ of this *Shin*.

ORDER OF INSERTION

1st. **Tai**—Camellia bud.
2nd. **Tai tani**—Full-blown camellia.
3rd. **Tai shin**—Branch with bud and flower.
4th. **Shin mae**—Willow branch.
5th. **Shin**—Willow branch.

IKE-NO-BO

Gyakugatte or Left Hand Arrangement.

An arrangement using branches of purple magnolia in a large basket.

Cut *Shin* 2½ times the height of the basket.

ORDER OF INSERTION IN KUBARI

1st.   **Tai**—Branch with bud.
2nd.   **Tani**—Branch with full-blown blossom.
3rd.   **Shin**—Branch with bud and half-open blossom.
4th.   **Maezoe**—Branch with bud and half-open blossom.
5th.   **Soe**—Branch with buds.

IKE-NO-BO

Tomari-fune or Standing Boat Arrangement.

This arrangement is made of but one spray of white camellia. The tallest bud spray is about twice the width of the boat. The second bud is used as the *Tai* branch. The full-blown blossom is the *Tani* while the outstanding leaf at the right becomes the *Soe* branch.

IKE-NO-BO

Gyakugatte Tachi-no-bori or Left Hand Arrangement.

An arrangement of flowering Japanese quince.

TO MAKE

Cut *Shin* twice the height of the container.
Cut *Soe* ⅔ the height of the *Shin*.
Cut *Tai* ⅓ the height of the *Shin*.

ORDER OF INSERTION IN KUBARI

1st.	Tai.
2nd.	Tai tani.
3rd.	Shin mae.
4th.	Shin.
5th.	Shin ushiro.
6th.	Maezoe.
7th.	Soe.

Hongatte De-fune or Outgoing Boat Arrangement.

An arrangement of iris in a hanging boat—the long leaves sweeping off to the right suggest to the Japanese the single long oar which they use to propel their boats.

Select your longest flower-bud and leaf group—carefully re-arrange and bend into desired shape—the two lower leaves become the " *Nagashi*," while the flower bud and the leaf above it comprise the *Tai* group of this arrangement. Use full-blown flower for *Tani*.

Always keep the tips of the main part of the arrangement well within the triangle formed by the supporting chains, and the tip of the *Shin* directly under its apex.

ORDER OF INSERTION IN KUBARI

1st. **Tai**—Insert *Nagashi* and *Tai* group of one bud and three leaves.
2nd. **Tani**—Full-blown flower.
3rd. **Shin mae**—Flower-bud and two leaves.
4th. **Shin**—Long leaf.
5th. **Soe**—Leaf about ⅔ the height of the *Shin* leaf.

NOTE :—To bend leaves and flower stems into desired shape wet both leaves and fingers with clean cold water and gently coax into shape by drawing leaves through the fingers. Hold the leaf firm with the fingers on top of the leaf and exert pressure by the thumb underneath.

IKE-NO-BO

Gyakugatte Gyo-do-Ike or Left Hand "Fish-path" Arrangement.

A simple, but exceedingly pleasing arrangement of but two iris blossoms and their leaves.

Although an *Ike-no-bo* arrangement, a *kubari* is not used. One large *kenzan* will suffice.

ORDER OF INSERTION

1st. Shin group :—Cut bud 1½ times the width of the container, add leaf just a little shorter, inside the *kenzan*, upright.

2nd. Shin ushiro :—Use a leaf a little shorter than *Shin* leaf, insert to right of *Shin*.

3rd. Shin mae :—Leaf shorter than *Shin ushiro*, insert to left and closely following the line of *Shin*.

4th. Soe group :—Use full-blown flower, cut ⅔ height of *Shin*. Insert to right of *Shin*—add one long leaf to right, give this leaf a slight curve. Now add second leaf.

5th. Tai group :—Arrange three leaves as per illustration and insert in *kenzan* to the left and a little separate from the *Shin* and *Soe* groups.

146

IKE-NO-BO

Gyakugatte or Left Hand Arrangement.

An arrangement of common yellow lilies in an "*Ogencho*", a bronze vase used only for *Ike-no-bo* arrangements.

TO MAKE

Use flowers and leaves in natural groupings—though it may be necessary to strip off some of the outside shorter leaves.

Cut *Shin* 2 ½ times the height of the vase and follow the usual proportions for *Ike-no-bo*.

ORDER OF INSERTION IN KUBARI

1st.   Tai.
2nd.   Shin mae.
3rd.   Shin.
4th.   Shin ushiro.
5th.   Soe.

IKE-NO-BO

Gyakugatte or Left Hand Arrangement.

An arrangement of wild aster in typical iron vase. An example of one of the many cases where the natural growth of the plant material used influences the arrangement. Because of the wild aster's growing habit the flowers used are exceptionally tall—the leaves conform to the usual *Ike-no-bo* proportions.

TO MAKE

Cut one flower stalk 4 times the height of the container—this is the *Shin* flower.

Cut second flower ⅔ the height of the *Shin* flower—this is the *Soe* flower.

Now select a fine large leaf—cut it 1½ times the height of the container. This is the *Shin* leaf. Cut six others according to usual *Ike-no-bo* proportions.

ORDER OF INSERTION IN KUBARI

1st.   Tai leaf.
2nd.   Tai no Tani leaf.
3rd.   Shin mae leaf.
4th.   Shin leaf.
5th.   Shin flower.
6th.   Soe flower.
7th.   Shin no ushiro leaf.
8th.   Soe leaf.
9th.   Ushirozoe leaf.

NOTE :—Gently bend into shape after the leaves are fastened in the *kubari*.

Iri-fune or Incoming Boat Arrangement.

An arrangement of a single morning glory with vine tendrils and leaves. Make the *Nagashi* (long drooping branch) about the length of the boat; keep the *Shin* branch well within the angle made by the supporting strings. A rusted pin pierced through the end of the stem will help to prolong the life of this flower.

IKE-NO-BO

Hongatte or Right Hand Arrangement.

An arrangement of kaffir corn and small white chrysanthemums in a sage green porcelain bowl. In the composition *Shin* and *Shin-ushiro* are on the same stalk; if your material will not admit of that, a second stalk may be added. Conform as closely as possible to the picture, no matter how many stalks are necessary. Cut *Shin* 2½ times the height of the bowl, and other parts to usual *Ike-no-bo* proportions. Note that the *Soe* leaf is allowed to droop; this is in harmony with the nature of the plant, as well as producing a beautiful variation of line.

The small white chrysanthemums used grow naturally in clusters or bunches, therefore suggest this by keeping part of the arrangement full and bunchy, taking care, however, to make it crescent shaped, not round.

ORDER OF INSERTION

1st.   **Tai** —Small white chrysanthemum.

2nd.   **Tai tani**—Small white chrysanthemum.

3rd.   **Tai shin mae**—Small white chrysanthemum.

4th.   **Tai shin**—Small white chrysanthemum.

5th.   **Shin mae**—Use two stalks of the kaffir corn, cut off most of the large leaves and make remaining ones conform closely to the line of the stem.

6th.   **Shin**—Long, strong stalk of kaffir corn with second grain head attached. Discard all but one large sweeping leaf.

7th.   **Soe**—Stalk of kaffir corn—strip off all but one large leaf.

IKE-NO-BO

Hongatte Ni-ju no Ike-no-bo or Double Arrangement.

An arrangement of *sonare*, a kind of cypress and small chrysanthemums of two sizes and colours, in a bamboo container of traditional shape.

TO MAKE UPPER ARRANGEMENT

SHIN GROUP :—Cut branch of cypress equal to total height of the container and bend into the shape of the *Soe* branch of the regular *Ike-no-bo* arrangement. Two smaller branches are necessary to complete this group.

SOE GROUP :—Cut branch of the cypress ⅔ the length of *Shin* and bend into the shape of the *Shin* branch of the regular *Ike-no-bo* arrangements. Two smaller branches are necessary to complete this group.

NEJIME :—Cut three sprays of small pink chrysanthemums and arrange according to shape of *Nejime* of regular *Ike-no-bo*.

ORDER OF INSERTION

1st. **Tai**—Branch of chrysanthemum.
2nd. **Tani**—Branch of chrysanthemum.
3rd. **Tai shin**—Branch of chrysanthemum.
4th. **Shin mae**—Branch of cypress.
5th. **Shin**—Branch of cypress.
6th. **Shin ushiro**—Branch of cypress.
7th. **Maezoe**—Branch of cypress.
8th. **Soe**—Branch of cypress.
9th. **Ushirozoe**—Branch of cypress.

TO MAKE LOWER ARRANGEMENT

Use larger yellow chrysanthemums and make a simple *Shin-Soe-Tai* arrangement, keeping well within the opening in the container.

ORDER OF INSERTION

1st. **Tai**—Chrysanthemum.
2nd. **Shin**—Chrysanthemum.
3rd. **Soe**—Chrysanthemum.

IKE-NO-BO

Gyakugatte or Left Hand Arrangement.

An arrangement of "*Omoto*"—green sword-like leaves with red berries.

Although this is one of the old traditional *Ike-no-bo* arrangements, an even number of leaves is used and it is arranged in any flat container. It is shown here arranged in a grey hand-made pottery dish on a red lacquer stand.

The terms for the different parts of this arrangement are slightly different from those used for the usual *Ike-no-bo* arrangements. *Shin mae* becomes *Tachi ba*, *Tai* becomes *Tsuyu uke ba*, and *Tai shin* becomes *Nagashi no ha*.

TO MAKE

Use longest leaf for *Shin* and do not cut, also retain one long leaf for *Nagashi no ha*. Arrange as a *Moribana* in the following order :

1st.	**Shin.**	5th.	**Tachi ba.**
2nd.	**Shin ushiro.**	6th.	**Tsuyu uke ba.**
3rd.	**Soe.**	7th.	**Nagashi no ha.**
4th.	**Ushirozoe.**	8th.	Leaf behind **Nagashi no ha.**

NOTE :—Now insert branch of berries in the middle of the arrangement so that it appears to be surrounded by the two *Nagashi no ha* and the *Tsuyu uke ba*. Two groups of berries are never used, as this plant naturally produces but one each year.

IKE-NO-BO

Hongatte or Right Hand Arrangement.

An arrangement of plum branches and narcissus in a bronze vase.

TO MAKE

The natural shape of the branches is taken advantage of— very little bending is necessary.

Cut *Shin* 2½ times the height of the container, and follow usual proportions. This arrangement uses only four branches and two flowers, but the tips of the smaller branches furnish the desired odd number for the finished arrangement.

ORDER OF INSERTION IN KUBARI

1st.   **Tai.**—Use one narcissus with its leaves.
2nd.   **Tai-shin.**—Use second narcissus with its leaves.
3rd.   **Shin-mae.**—Use plum branch.
4th.   **Shin.**—Use plum branch.
5th.   **Shin-ushiro.**—Use plum branch.
6th.   **Soe.**—Use plum branch.

NOTE :—Sometimes the natural grouping of the narcissus, four leaves and stalk of blossoms, can be used, but it is often advisable to separate the groups and re-arrange.   In this arrangement the group used as *Tai* has been re-arranged so as to give a long sweeping line of leaf for the *Tai* branch and the blossom of this group has been used as the *Tani* or lowest point of the entire arrangement.

IKE-NO-BO

Gyakugatte or Left Hand Arrangement.

An arrangement of red berries and white chrysanthemums in an old bronze container, "Sunabachi".

For this type of container a heavy lead ring is used to hold the flowers. Insert *kubari* in this ring and place it in the centre of the container—proceed to arrange as simple *Ike-no-bo*. In the composition, *Shin* and *Shin-ushiro* are on the same stem—if using other material it may be necessary to add a separate branch for *Shin-ushiro*. Also the *Soe* and *Maezoe* branches are together; it may be necessary to add a second branch here. Cut *Shin* about twice the width of the container and other branches according to usual *Ike-no-bo* proportions.

ORDER OF INSERTION

1st. **Tai.**—Leaf branch of camellia.
2nd. **Tai tani.**—Camellia branch with bud and full-blown blossom.
3rd. **Tai shin.**—Camellia branch with half-open flower.
4th. **Shin.**—Which includes *Maezoe* branch of red berries.
5th. **Soe.**—Use plum branch.

NOTE :—Cover holder with large water-worn stones.

IKE-NO-BO

Kakebana.

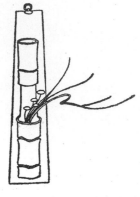

Pussy willow and small white chrysanthemums in a bamboo hanging container.

In this arrangement use has been made of an odd-shaped branch of the pussy willow for the *Soe* branch. In an arrangement like this, proportion is of the utmost importance. In cutting branches, it is the apparent height, or length, of branches that is to be considered. Flower arrangement is an art and exact measurements cannot be given. Bear in mind the *Ike-no-bo* proportions of thirds. Note that in this arrangement the apparent length of the *Soe* branch is approximately the total length of the container, the height of the *Shin* branch is approximately ⅔ the height of the *Soe* branch, and that the *Tai* group stays well within the opening in the bamboo container and is approximately ⅓ of the *Soe* branch. The *Tai* group should point directly forward, neither to the right nor to the left. The charm of this arrangement depends entirely on beauty of line—do not use too many willow branches or flowers.

ORDER OF INSERTION

1st. **Tai** group of 7 chrysanthemums; bear in mind the usual shape for *Nejime*.

2nd. **Shin mae**—Shortest willow branch.

3rd. **Shin**—Willow branch.

4th. **Shin ushiro**—Willow branch.

5th. **Soe**—Willow branch.

164

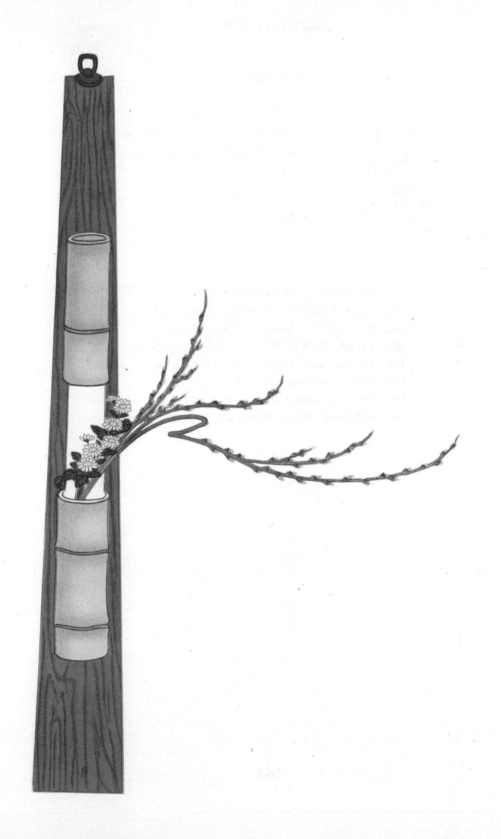

IKE-NO-BO

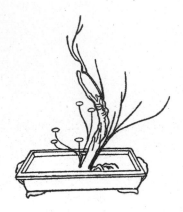

Gyakugatte or Left Hand Arrangement.

Pussy willow and small yellow chrysan-themums in *Sunabachi*—showing use of large willow limb, and stones to give a sense of stability.

Cut *Shin* a generous 2½ times the width of the container.

ORDER OF INSERTION

1st. **Tai**—Branch of chrysanthemum.

2nd. **Tai tani**—Branch of chrysanthemum.

3rd. **Tai shin mae**—Branch of chrysanthemum.

4th. **Tai shin**—Branch of chrysanthemum.

5th. **Tai shin ushiro.**—Branch of chrysanthemum.

6th. **Shin**—Large branch of willow.

7th. **Soe**—Long slender branch of willow.

8th. **Ushirozoe**—Willow branch, part of which serves as *maezoe.*

SHO-FU-RYU MORIBANA

MORIBANA is an informal arrangement. Unlike *Ike-no-bo*, where skill of arrangement and beauty of line are of paramount importance, *Moribana* lays stress on naturalness. Very little bending of branches is allowed in this style of arrangement.

The laws governing any Japanese flower arrangement presuppose an intimate knowledge of plant growth on the part of the arranger. Flowers that grow naturally on the plains are never indiscriminately arranged with those that grow on the mountains, nor are water plants ever combined with flowers that grow in dry places. Field and garden flowers are never combined, nor

171

flowers of different seasons.   A plant that grows naturally at the foot of a tree must not be given a higher position than a tree branch, but must occupy a lower position.   Branches of a tree are arranged with the base free from foliage to suggest the trunk of a tree—but bush branches are arranged with foliage so that the stems are hidden by short branches of the same material to suggest a growing bush.

Far fewer flowers are used in a Japanese arrangement than in the usual European, but each flower is shown to its best advantage. Buds rather than full-blown flowers are used.   Flowers out of season are to be avoided; if used they must be used sparingly to show that they are not easily obtainable.

The season of the year governs the density of the arrangement :—*Moribana* should always represent nature at the time of arrangement. Only in Summer are flowers used profusely; at other times tree branches and even grasses are used together with a few flowers.   One form of *Moribana* arrangements expresses a bit of nature—a quiet garden—a corner in a forest—flowers growing by

172

the side of a lake; another form known as *shikisai* or colour combination uses cut flowers in profusion for colour effects.

Expensive containers are not necessary—the Japanese prefer baskets in their natural colours, or neutral coloured hand-made pottery or bronze containers for their arrangements, according to the plant material used. Boxes and covered jars are often used and their lids considered as part of the arrangement. In this case small porcelain or bamboo containers are placed inside the box to hold the water and flowers.

Colour harmony between flowers used and container is very important. An odd-shaped container will often totally change the effect of very common flowers, giving them an unsuspected beauty. Any and all flowers and tree branches may be arranged this way to great advantage if care is taken in the selection of the container. Any number of flowers and any number of colours is permissible in *Moribana*.

Never fill the whole container; always allow at least half clear of flowers, showing only the water. To the Japanese this is quite the normal way; a flower arrangement to them is not just a display of cut flowers; it must suggest some natural bit of scenery or landscape, and a Japanese landscape or garden without water or its suggestion is unthinkable.

In selecting a container for certain flowers, or flowers for a favourite container, bear in mind the *Moribana* proportions of once and a half to twice the width of the container for the *Shin* or longest branch. Do not attempt to arrange a large flower in a small container, or a small flower in one much too large for it. There is an exception to this rule. The Japanese love a long narrow square or oblong container which on first consideration might appear suitable for a large flower, but actually small flowers, such as water-lilies, cyclamen, or compositions of ribbon grass appear in it to good advantage. In such a case great care is necessary for the proper placement of the flower group in the container, usually about a quarter of the way from the end is best ; the surface of the water is considered an important part of the composition. See illustration, page 227.

Any plant material may be used. The Japanese prefer to use flowering branches of trees or evergreens with appropriate flowers of contrasting colours.

After suitable combination of plant material and colour harmony, proportion is to be considered. In deciding the length of branches to be used, both the place of display and size of container, including stand on which it is to be displayed, must be considered.

Flower arrangement is an art and art cannot be confined to arbitrary limits ; however, a safe rule is, after deciding the height of the main *Shin* branch make all other branches in proportion to that. To determine the height of this *Shin* branch, consideration must be given to the nature of the plant material used, container, and place where arrangement is to be displayed. Do not be afraid to make a tall slender arrangement—such arrangements are graceful and more pleasing than low squat compositions. Avoid crowding many flowers into a small space—allow each branch or blossom to be seen to its best advantage.

Sho-fu-ryu Moribana adheres to the proportions used for so many years in the *Ike-no-bo* school of arrangement—namely thirds. The length of *Shin* is determined by the container used; *Soe* is $^2/_3$ and *Tai* $^1/_2$ the length of *Shin*. Note the resemblance of these three groups—*Shin, Soe, Tai*, to the same groups of the *Ike-no-bo* arrangements.

Measurements are given for the apparent or finished lengths. Weak and slender tips are not considered, only the strong part is measured.

Always cut first the branch behind the main branch of any group, then the branch in front.

175

There are various kinds of *Moribana*, determined both by the shape of the container and the plant material. Every branch or flower naturally has a back and a front. In deciding how to arrange any given branch or flower consider the angle at which it can be seen to best advantage.

Ike-no-bo is the basic foundation of all schools of flower arrangement. As you remember, we worked with groups of three, or rather sets of branches in threes, each in itself forming a triangular arrangement. This same idea is carried out in *Moribana*.

In any *Moribana* arrangement there are six groups: These groups may be made up of any number of flowers or branches.

Shin Group, which includes *Mikoshi*.

Soe Group.

Tai Group.

Tani Group.

Do Group.

Tome Group.

Sho-fu-ryu Moribana is based on the traditional Japanese arrangement which has come down through the ages ; to the basic trinity of *Shin*, *Soe*, *Tai*, three more branches or groups of branches are added. For best results it is well to keep in mind the curves of *Shin*, *Soe* and *Tai* of the *Ike-no-bo*, and to adapt the added branches to them. The heights of the main branches of *Shin*, *Soe*, *Tai* groups are determined, as is also that of one of the new branches, the *Tome*; the others, however, are left to the good judgement and skill of the arranger.

Mikoshi :—Is the name applied to one or more branches or flowers placed a little to one side of the *Shin* branch, which serve to create a false perspective and widen the arrangement.

Mikoshi is a garden term and means " to see over "—there

176

should be a taller branch in front of the *Mikoshi* over which the viewer must look.

Do means "body" and is one or more branches or flowers added to thicken the composition and to tie the three main groups together.

Tome means "stopper"—it is placed just behind and a little to one side of *Shin*, always on the opposite side to the *Mikoshi* branch; it creates a false horizon line, or the idea of a boundary line to a garden. It serves to balance the arrangement; without it the composition seems to be toppling forward. *Tome* may consist of one or more flowers or branches.

Tani means "valley"; another garden term borrowed for flower arrangement. It is always the lowest group in the composition, and is necessary to give a sense of stability; it hides the base of the stems of the main branches and the *kenzan* (holders).

As with *Ike-no-bo*, consider yourself as the sun and arrange flowers as if growing naturally. Remember that flowers always show their best sides to the sun and reach out towards it. Use buds or light-coloured flowers for the *Shin-Soe-Tai* main branches and full-blown or dark flowers for the *Do* and *Tani*. For *Mikoshi* and *Tome* use half-open flowers, tight buds, or leaves only, accord ing to plant material.

The tips of all branches or flowers must face upwards as if to catch the dew; do not allow them to droop.

Measurements are given for all main branches, but it should be borne in mind that these are only approximate; they will vary with the plant material. In dealing with so sentient and individualistic a material as flowers no hard and fast rules can be laid down, but at the same time there are certain limits within which one must work if the most harmonious results are desired.

The arrangement is said to be a right hand (*Hongatte*) one if the *Tai* branch points to the right, and a left hand one (*Gyakugatte*) if the *Tai* branch points to the left; though the flowers actually are on the left of the container in a *Hongatte* arrangement, and on the right side of the container in a *Gyakugatte* arrangement.

A minute's extra care in covering the flower holder in the

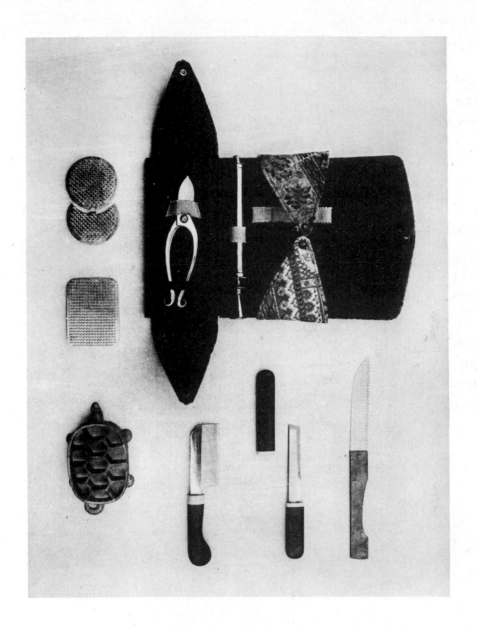

Case for holding tools used in flower arrangement; and flower holders.

most natural manner will repay the effort. Do not lay plant material flat in the water ; arrange as if growing upright, not as if floating dead on the water. This may seem an unimportant point, but actually it can make or mar the arrangement. A Japanese flower arrangement according to the Japanese method must express living growth.

Moribana requires a large flat dish or basket and *kenzan*. *Kenzan* are lead blocks of needles in which flowers are stuck and held upright. Holders with round or irregularly shaped holes can be used ; but to incline the branch or flower is more difficult; they must be held in place by wedges of plant material. If *kenzan* are not available, a potato or other large heavy vegetable may be used ; or B.B. shot or small pebbles can be put in the bottom of the container and the branches stuck into them.

Always stand squarely in front of the container, and face all flowers towards you, as if you were the sun towards which all flowers turn naturally.

Keep in mind that each group is complete in itself, and a harmonious part of the entire arrangement.

In the following diagrams the groups are represented by a single line and only the indispensable branches are indicated. Sometimes a spreading branch of plant material will contain in itself two or more groups, sometimes several branches are necessary for one group, depending on the plant material used.

GENERAL INSTRUCTIONS FOR ANY
MORIBANA ARRANGEMENT

A *Moribana* arrangement can be made of any plant materials appropriately combined. Usually an odd number of kinds is preferred; other than two an even number of kinds is never used. The Japanese prefer tree or bush branches for the *Shin* and *Soe* groups, though these groups are never kept distinctly separated— flowers used in the *Tai* group will be introduced into these groups to bind the entire arrangement into unity.

If flowers only are used (as for dining table decoration), two or more flowers may be used for each different group. Never have two flowers of equal size or colour, or two flowers of the same height; the Japanese way is to have always medium, high and low. If three or more flowers of any distinctive colour are used see that they are not only uneven in height but that they form the points of a colour triangle in the arrangement.

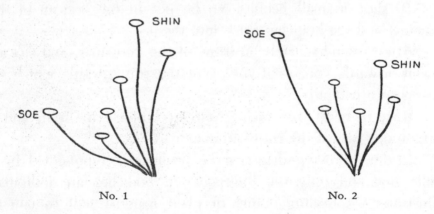

No. 1   No. 2

Diagram No. 1 shows the usual proportions between the *Shin* and *Soe* groups, with *Soe* $^2/_3$ the height of the *Shin*.

Diagram No. 2 shows a variation of these proportions wherein *Shin* is $^2/_3$ the height of *Soe*. This is often advisable in a *Kansui-ike* arrangement.

In any style of arrangement an effect of steps should be avoided. Diagram No. 3 is incorrect—an arrangement based on these proportions would be monotonous.

182

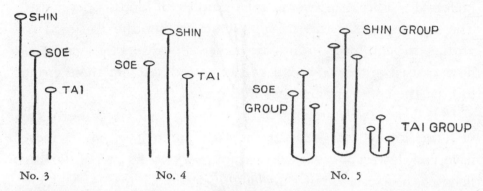

No. 3   No. 4   No. 5

Diagrams No. 4 and No. 5 show a correct spacing of the different heights, harmonious and most pleasing to the eye.

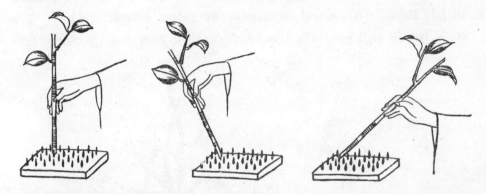

Generally speaking, for a *Hongatte* (right hand) arrangement the main *Shin* branch stands upright; the *Soe* branch leans to the left; and the *Tai* branch extends well to the front and just the least bit to the right. If these general positions are kept in mind, together with the general proportions of container and main branches, to arrange flowers in the Japanese way becomes a joy.

For a *Gyakugatte* (left hand) arrangement the main *Shin* branch retains its upright position, but the *Soe* branch leans to the right and the *Tai* branch the least bit to the left.

183

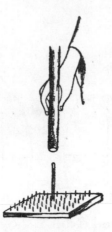

To arrange a hollow stemmed lily, such as amaryllis, calla, etc., cut branch, or even strong splinter of wood, and insert in hollow of lily stem, then stand in *kenzan* or other flower holder. The stick inside will keep the lily from drooping or falling over.

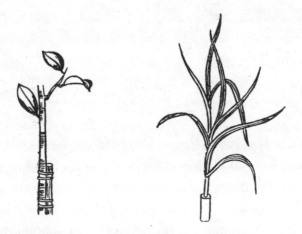

To arrange slender-stemmed flowers or leaves. Cut to length and bind piece of other and larger plant material to it—taking care to fasten it twice, as pictured; or insert end of slender stem in larger stem of hollow or soft plant material.

184

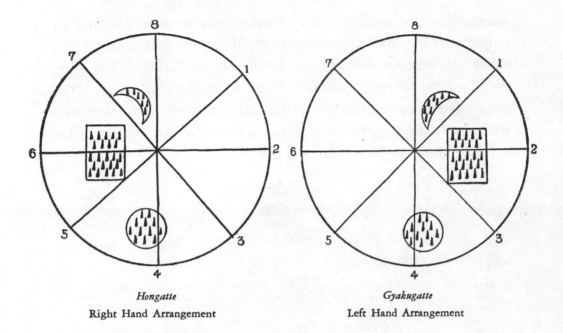

Hongatte
Right Hand Arrangement

Gyakugatte
Left Hand Arrangement

While the diagram represents a round container, any shape may be used, of course. It is not necessary actually to draw the lines; but imagine your container crossed by four lines, one of which is exactly perpendicular to you, dividing the surface of the water into eight equal parts. Imagine the points of intersection of the lines with the rim of your container numbered from 1 to 8 clockwise. It is these points that are of importance in the following instructions. The centre point, or point of intersection of all these lines is not of importance, except to be avoided in a Japanese flower arrangement.

The small round, square and crescent-shaped diagrams represent *kenzan* or lead blocks of needles to hold the flowers. Any kind of holder may be substituted; but they should be placed in the same relative positions in the container. It is not always necessary to use three *kenzan*; sometimes one is sufficient, some-

185

times several are necessary, but in general the position remains the same ; note that half the container is left free from flowers.   The entire arrangement should not extend beyond Lines 3 and 8 for the *Hongatte* arrangement, and 5 and 8 for the *Gyakugatte*.   The *kenzan* determine the position of the base or root ends of the flowers which are close together as if growing naturally but the tips of the different branches take various positions.

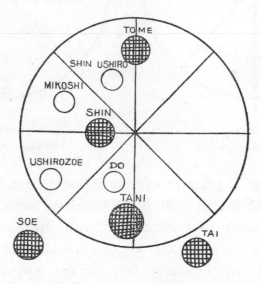

The diagram above shows the positions of the tips of the main branches for a *Hongatte*, or right hand arrangement—the *Gyakugatte* is the reverse.

186

GENERAL INSTRUCTIONS FOR MAKING ANY MORIBANA ARRANGEMENT

FIRST STEP—SHIN GROUP

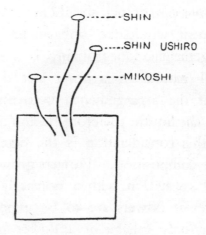

Showing position of *Shin* Group.

Select tall slender strong-tipped branch, or flower bud if only flowers are to be used. Cut once and a half to twice the diameter of the container and gently bend into a curve approximating that of the *Shin* branch of an *Ike-no-bo* arrangement. Insert in square *kenzan* well to the rear so as to allow room for the *Soe*, *Do* and *Tani* groups.

The tip of the *Shin* branch should always be over its base, though the branch itself need not be straight. If using flowers see that all leaves point upwards and follow the line of the stem. If using branch material the small twigs should have their tips pointing upwards, and as a rule a branch leaving the main stem at a right-angle is avoided. If using plant material which has flowers

187

or twigs branching off at the same joint, cut off one of them, retaining the one whose line conforms to the main stem.

Now, whether using branches or flowers, make this group fairly complete in itself; add branches or flowers keeping in mind that there should be at least one branch in the rear of the *Shin* branch, *Shin-ushiro*, but that it should not be very full.

This *Shin-ushiro* branch should never be neglected—without it the arrangement would be unbalanced—and while a Japanese flower arrangement unquestionably is a one-point-of-view composition, still naturalism is never lost sight of. The *Shin* is the centre of the arrangement; between it and the viewer is considered as the South, therefore behind *Shin* is considered as the North, and this consideration is the determining factor for the density of the composition. Flowers grow naturally to the South, and naturally vegetation with a northerly exposure grows more slowly and fewer flowers are to be expected. Therefore *Shin-ushiro* is often only foliage or a flower bud; sometimes a seed pod or imperfect leaf used in this position will add great interest to an otherwise insipid composition. Never use perfect blossoms in this position.

The *Mikoshi* branch or flower is placed in front of the *Shin* branch or flower, always on the opposite side to that of the *Shin-ushiro*. This branch serves to widen the composition and is best made of foliage or flower bud because its object is to produce the illusion of perspective, and even a full-blown flower seen in the distance would appear small—therefore use a bud or small flower. The *Shin-mae* (before *Shin*) branch or flower should be cut about $2/3$ the height of the main branch. Remember it is the apparent or finished height that we are considering, not the actual measurements in inches.

SECOND STEP—SOE GROUP

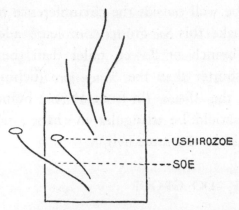

USHIROZOE

SOE

Diagram showing completed *Shin* Group and position of *Soe* Group.

Look over your material and if possible select a branch or flower with a curve approximating the curve of the *Soe* branch of the *Ike-no-bo* arrangement, or bend one to desired shape. Cut about ²/₃ the height of the *Shin* branch. For most flowers it will be sufficient to insert in *kenzan* at the proper angle—as a rule flowers are used without any bending—though it is possible to curve the stem the least bit so that it will balance a heavy flower upright. Always be sure that the blossom on the end of its stem faces upwards as though to catch and hold the dew. If using branch material see that the extreme tip curves upwards slightly, to express growth. Never allow a blossom or tip of any branch to droop (except of course, in cases where the flower blossom naturally grows that way, which is not often).

Whether using flower or branch material, trim off all downward reaching flowers or twigs from the under side of the *Soe* branch ; this is important. Gently bend and twist all leaves and small twigs to conform with the line of the main stem. Insert well to the front and to the left side of the square *kenzan* and extend the main *Soe* branch out over Line 5. The tip of the branch will be well outside the circumference of the container.

Now make this *Soe* group complete ; add first the *Ushiro-zoe* (behind *Soe*) branch or flower, taller than the *Mikoshi* branch or flower but shorter than the *Shin-ushiro* (behind *Shin*) branch or flower, then the *Maezoe* (in front of *Soe*) branch in front of *Soe*. This group should be triangular in shape ; no two branches or flowers should be the same height.

THIRD STEP—DO GROUP

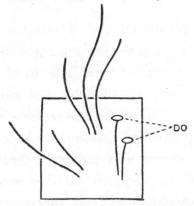

Diagram showing completed *Shin* and *Soe* Groups and position of *Do* Group.

The heights of this group are not fixed, they will vary with every arrangement according to the plant material used ; often a special branch or flower for *Do* will be necessary ; sometimes the *Shin* and *Soe* groups are sufficient without it ; *Do* means " body " and is merely a thickening of the main central part of the composition.

Insert in square *kenzan* in front of *Shin* to the right of the *Soe* groups.

FOURTH STEP—TAI and TANI GROUPS

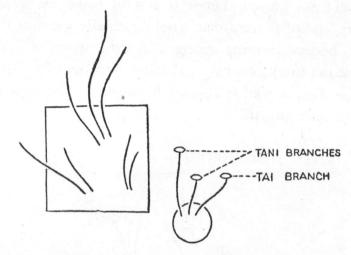

TANI BRANCHES

TAI BRANCH

Diagram showing completed *Shin*, *Soe* and *Do* Groups, and
position of the *Tai* and *Tani* Groups.

Use round *kenzan*.   Sometimes the entire arrangement can
be inserted in the one *kenzan*, sometimes several are necessary, but
as a rule the three pictured in the diagram on page 185 are
necessary for best results.   Select a branch with a vigorous tip or
flower bud for the *Tai* branch.   Cut about ⅓ the height of *Shin*.
Insert *Tai* branch or flower in the round *kenzan* with its tip extending
out over the rim of the container between Lines 3 and 4.   The *Tai*
group is triangular, with its lowest point in the centre (the
opposite of the *Shin* group which has its highest point in the centre).

Tani or " valley " is almost always necessary ; it is the
lowest group of the entire arrangement and brings it into optical
stability.   *Tani* also serves to hide the stem ends of the flowers or
branches and to cover the holders in which they are inserted.

If using flowers, full-blown or dark-coloured (or both) are
most suitable for *Tani*.

191

If using tree branches *Do* can be of the same material as the *Shin* and *Soe* groups, but it is best to make the *Tani* group of flowers, and of flowers that would naturally grow at the foot of a tree, because in many arrangements the stems of *Shin* and *Soe* suggest the trunk of a tree. If using branches of a bush for *Shin* and *Soe*, *Tani* as well as *Do* may be made of the same material to suggest bush growth.

FIFTH STEP—TOME GROUP

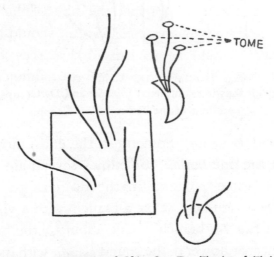

Diagram showing completed *Shin*, *Soe*, *Do*, *Tani* and *Tai* Groups
and position of the *Tome* Group.

This group goes into the crescent-shaped *kenzan*, a little to the rear of the *Shin* group. Its purpose is to bring the eye to rest and to balance the composition. Either branch material or flowers can be used for this group. Cut main branch or flower about half the length of the main *Shin* branch and insert in *kenzan* upright but with its stem following the line of the *Shin* stem.

Make this group triangular in shape but keep it scant. Being at the rear of *Shin* it is considered as subject to a northern exposure, therefore perfect branches or full-blown flowers are not suitable.   Use a tight bud or imperfect blossom with few or imperfect leaves for this group.   Do not hesitate to cut and trim plant material for this group; without it the composition is unbalanced, but if it is too profuse it only adds confusion.

Check over your finished arrangement.   Make sure that you have an odd number of branches or flower tips where one branch has been used for two or more groups.   Cut off any unnecessary or confusing branches that obstruct the line of the stems.   The tips of the three main branches, *Shin-Soe-Tai*, should form a triangle and your flowers should be so massed that they form a colour triangle.   The stem lines of the three main branches should be easily traceable.

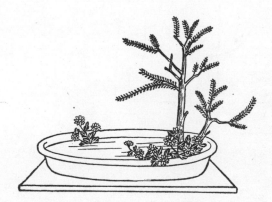

Cut off all small branches, leaves and even flowers to expose the line of the stems.   If large tree branches have been used see that they suggest the trunk of a tree, and are not hidden by foliage or flowers.   If bush branches are used there should be a few short branches hiding the main large stems to suggest a bush.   Keep each different kind of branch material separate in *kenzan* with roots close together to suggest a tree or bush, and use small plant material to tie the groups of the composition together as nature does.

To hide the *kenzan* or any other holder use club moss if available ; if it is not, use leaves from the foliage of the arrangement.   Do not make this part of the arrangement too obvious, make it as natural-looking as possible—a surprisingly small amount of moss or other foliage will completely hide the holders.

SIMPLE MORIBANA

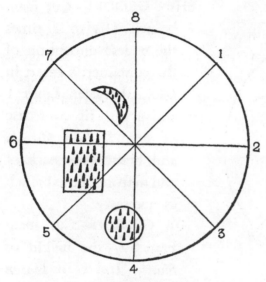

Showing positions of *kenzan* for *Hongatte* or Right Hand Arrangement.

SHIN GROUP:—Cut main branch $1\frac{1}{2}$ to 2 times the widest dimension of the container. Insert in *kenzan* between Lines 6 and 7 with tip over its base. Add branches in back of and in front of main branch as necessary.

SOE GROUP:—Cut main branch $\frac{2}{3}$ the height of *Shin* and insert in *kenzan* on Line 6 with tip extending over Line 5. Add branches in back of and in front of this branch as necessary.

DO GROUP:—There is no fixed height for this group, sometimes it is not necessary.

TAI GROUP:—Cut main branch $\frac{1}{3}$ the height of *Shin* and insert in *kenzan* on Line 4 with tip extending between Lines 3 and 4. Add necessary branches between this main branch and the *Shin* group.

TANI GROUP:—No fixed height.

TOME GROUP:—Cut main branch $\frac{1}{2}$ the height of *Shin* and insert in *kenzan* between Lines 7 and 8 with tip over its base. Add necessary branches in front of this main branch.

195

SIMPLE MORIBANA

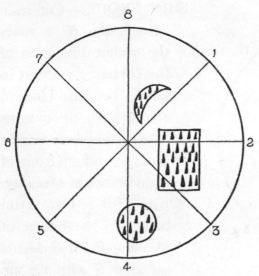

Showing positions of *kenzan* for *Gyakugatte*, or Left Hand Arrangement.

SHIN GROUP:—Cut main branch $1\frac{1}{2}$ to 2 times the widest dimension of the container. Insert in *kenzan* between Lines 1 and 2 with tip over base of stem. Add *Mikoshi* and branches in back of and in front of this branch as necessary.

SOE GROUP:—Cut main branch $\frac{2}{3}$ the height of *Shin*. Insert in *kenzan* on Line 2 with tip extending over Line 3. Add branches in back of and in front of this branch as necessary.

DO GROUP:—There is no fixed height for this group, sometimes it is not necessary.

TAI GROUP:—Cut main branch $\frac{1}{3}$ the height of *Shin* and insert in *kenzan* on Line 4 with tip extending between Lines 4 and 5. Add any necessary branches between this branch and the *Shin* group.

TANI GROUP:—There is no fixed height for this group, it is the lowest in the entire arrangement.

TOME GROUP:—Cut main branch $\frac{1}{2}$ the height of *Shin*, insert in *kenzan* between Lines 1 and 8, and add branches as necessary in front of the main branch.

196

SAMPLE LESSON

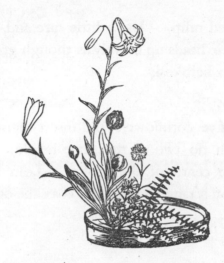

For a sample lesson we will make a *Shikisai* or " colour harmony " arrangement, and you will need :—

    2 Easter lilies,

    2 Red tulips,

    5 Blue cornflowers (or bachelor's buttons),

    3 Jonquils,

    Several leaves of the sword fern.

SHIN GROUP

Cut the longest Easter lily $1^1/_2$ times the diameter of the container, insert in *kenzan* as per diagram on page 187. This should stand upright with flowers showing to best advantage.

Mikoshi.—use red tulip. Insert in *kenzan* a little to the left and rear of the *Shin* lily ; lean slightly away from *Shin*.

SOE GROUP

Cut the second lily $^2/_3$ the length of the first and insert in

197

kenzan at a slant so that the tip is over Line 5.

DO GROUP

Insert second red tulip.   Use a little care and the tulips can be made to hold their heads up bravely as though growing; do not allow them to droop helplessly.

TANI GROUP

Now take the five cornflowers and insert them in the *kenzan* in a low group with no two of the same height.   Put the full blown flowers in the centre of the group.   Lean them all a bit towards you.   Cut off scraggly leaves and coax the others to follow the line of the stem.

TAI GROUP

Take three of the longest fern leaves and fasten them together—cut the length of the longest $1/3$ of *Shin*.   Insert this group in the small round *kenzan* leaning well forward so that the tip is over Line 3.   Now add four more fern leaves, all of different lengths, so as to make a group of seven fern leaves.   The longest of the first group of three fern leaves is the *Tai*, and all the others must be shorter.   The shortest of the seven should go in the centre of the group.   Keep in mind the shape of the *Nejime* of the *Ike-no-bo* arrangement.

TOME GROUP

Separate the daffodils from the leaves ; rearrange with the leaves uneven in height, and fasten with wire so as to suggest a growing plant.

Cut these three groups all different lengths and insert in crescent-shaped *kenzan*, to the right of the *Shin* lily.

The finished arrangement should suggest a gay garden scene

in Spring, not just a bunch of flowers.   This lesson reflects the modern European influence on Japanese flower arrangement, for traditionally the Japanese are not fond of cut flowers, they wilt too quickly.   They prefer branches of a tree for the *Shin* and *Soe* groups, to suggest permanence and strength.   However, this is the simplest arrangement possible and the most useful.

It is but a suggestion; any similar flowers may be substituted.

FUTA-KABU

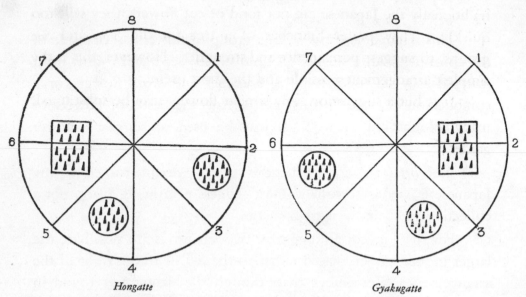

Hongatte   *Gyakugatte*

Showing placing of *kenzan* for *Futa-kabu Moribana* arrangement.

SHUZA OR LARGER GROUP

Shin :—Cut $1\frac{1}{2}$ to 2 times the widest dimension of the container.

Soe :—Cut $\frac{2}{3}$ of *Shin*.   *Tai* :—Cut $\frac{1}{3}$ of *Shin*.

Tome :—Cut $\frac{1}{2}$ of *Shin*.

Insert in *kenzan* as for simple *Moribana*, but make *Tai* scant. Keep this part of the arrangement well within Lines 4 and 7 for *Hongatte* (Right Hand Arrangement) or within Lines 1 and 4 for *Gyakugatte* (Left Hand Arrangement).

FUKUZA OR SMALLER GROUP

Shin :—Cut $\frac{3}{5}$ the length of *Shin* of larger group.

Soe :—Cut $\frac{2}{3}$ the length of *Shin* of this group.

Tai :—Cut $\frac{1}{3}$ the length of *Shin* of this group.

Tome :—Cut $\frac{1}{2}$ the length of *Shin* of this group.

200

SHO-FU-RYU FUTA-KABU MORIBANA

This arrangement has a large group of flowers on one side of the container with a smaller group distinctly separated. Any plant material may be used, but tree branches and small flowers, or a combination of water plants, are perhaps the best ; or flowers of many colours and many kinds may be used to suggest a flower garden.

Note that the arrangement is called " double-rooted "—any Japanese flower arrangement must suggest a growing plant, not a collection of cut flowers or branches.

For this kind of arrangement two variations are possible ; the larger group may be placed either to the left or to the right of the arrangement. Remember that, though the diagram is round in shape, any shape of container may be used. For this style of arrangement any rather large flat dish or basket is appropriate. Do not try to arrange a large branch or flower in too small a container. In selecting the container for any given flower keep in mind the *Moribana* proportions of once and a half to twice the width of the container for the tallest, or *Shin*, branch ; or if you plan to use a certain container select your flowers accordingly.

Place your *kenzan* or flower holders according to diagram on page 200, and follow rules for simple *Moribana*. Note that generally speaking the largest flower holder is (in a *Hongatte*) close to the left side of the container exactly in the centre of the width, and the largest group of the arrangement (*Shuza*) should be contained between the Lines 4 and 7, while the smaller group (*Fukuza*) should not extend beyond Lines 2 and 3. For the *Gyakugatte*, or the left hand arrangement, the positions are reversed, *Shuza*, or larger group, should be within the Lines 1 and 4, and *Fukuza*, or smaller group, between Lines 5 and 6.

The *Shin* of the smaller group (*Fukuza*) should be $3/5$ the height of the *Shin* of the larger group (*Shuza*). Each group is complete in itself, but the *Tai* group of the *Shuza* should be quite scant so as not to crowd the *Fukuza*. Follow diagrams for simple *Moribana*.

SHUZA :—Cut the *Shin* of the *Shuza* (larger group) $1\frac{1}{2}$ to 2 times the width of the container. Cut the *Soe* branch $2/3$ the height of the *Shin* and the *Tai* branch $1/3$ the height of the *Shin*. In simple *Moribana* the *Tai* extends to Line 3, but in this arrangement be careful to keep it pointing well forward, not extending beyond Line 4.

FUKUZA :—Cut *Shin* $5/6$ the height of the *Shin* of *Shuza* (larger group) and make a very scant arrangement with the *Tai* branch pointing towards the *Shuza* (larger group). This group should be complementary to the larger group and subordinate in every respect.

KANSUI-IKE MORIBANA

Kansui-ike, or " Water-viewing " arrangements can be made of any plant materials and are especially suitable for reeds and other water plants. Beautiful arrangements are possible of tree branches of interesting shapes combined with small water-loving plants. As their name implies, these arrangements should suggest a scene at the edge of a river or lake. Sometimes a dried branch of tree material can be combined with fresh green shrubs and water-seeking blossoms to produce the effect of an old dead tree by a river's side surrounded by fresh green vegetation.

Note that this style of arrangement is called *Hongatte* (Right Hand) when it is on the right side of the container with the *Tai* pointing to the left—in all other forms of arrangement the *Tai* determines whether the arrangement is right or left handed.

SOE GROUP

Select tree or bush branch of interesting shape ; or bend one to approximate the curve of the line in the diagram on page 206, and cut it the length of the diagonal of the container. Insert in *kenzan* with the tip of the branch extending from the right rear to the left front. Usually one branch is enough ; but if it is too scant and slender, or if a dried-up or moss-covered branch is used, add smaller branches (*Shin-ushiro* and *Shin-mae* in the diagram for simple *Moribana*) to simulate the new growth on an old tree. If using fresh green-leaved branches, cut off some of the leaves so as to show clearly the line of the main branch—do not have it evenly tapered off to its point—and be sure that the tip of the branch turns upwards as though growing.

SHIN GROUP

Use the same plant material as that used in the *Soe* group. Select slender strong-tipped branch, cut ²/₃ the length of *Soe*, or about twice the width of the container. Do not make this branch too tall; insert in *kenzan* upright with tip of branch over its base and make group complete by adding *Shin-ushiro*, *Shin-mae* and *Mikoshi* if necessary.

DO GROUP

Usually this is best composed of the same plant materials as the *Shin* and *Soe* groups; or it can be made of contrasting or harmonising materials. There is no fixed height for this branch; it must harmonise with and tie together the *Shin* and *Soe* groups.

TOME GROUP

Tome may be made of other materials than that of the *Shin* and *Soe* groups; often grass blades or wild orchid leaves are used to good effect; use bud if working with flowers—or half-open flower; never use a full-blown flower for this position. The main flower or branch should be half the height of the *Shin* branch. If more than one flower is used they should be of uneven heights.

TAI AND TANI GROUPS

These two groups are best made of other plant materials than that of the *Shin* and *Soe*, always of some low-growing plant or grass. Never use tree branches for the *Tani* group which is supposed to represent the vegetation found at the foot of a tree and is always the lowest part or shortest branch in the entire arrangement. Any number of kinds of low-growing plants may be used, depending on material at hand. Cut the *Tai* branch ¹/₃ the height

204

of *Shin*. Sometimes the same material as *Shin* and *Soe* is used for this branch. Insert in *kenzan* with tip extending about to Line 4—not beyond. Make the *Tani* group of some low-growing plant and insert in *kenzan*, keeping tips between Lines 2 and 3.

The *Gyakugatte*, or left hand arrangement, is the reverse of this.

Until skill is attained in the making of this arrangement it is well to use tree materials for *Shin*, *Soe* and *Tai*, and to make *Tome* and *Tani* of some low-growing plant material.

SHO-FU-RYU KANSUI-IKE MORIBANA

Water-Viewing Arrangement

Hongatte or Right Hand Arrangement.

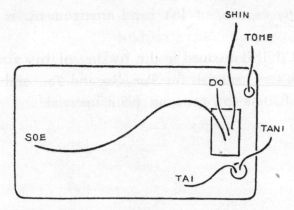

Showing positions of *kenzan* and main branches.

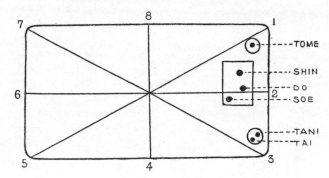

Showing positions of bases of main branches.

Order of Insertion

SOE GROUP:—Cut main branch equal to the length of the diagonal of the container and insert in *kenzan* below Line 2 so that tip of branch extends over Line 5.

SHIN GROUP :—Cut main branch $1\frac{1}{2}$ to 2 times the width of the container and insert upright in *kenzan* above Line 2.   Add necessary branches in back of and in front of this main branch.

DO GROUP :—There is no fixed height for this group ; sometimes it is not necessary.   If wanted, insert in *kenzan* between *Shin* and *Soe* main branches on Line 2.

TAI GROUP :—Cut main branch $\frac{1}{3}$ the height of *Shin* and insert in *kenzan* near Line 3 with tip extending towards Line 4.

TANI GROUP :—No fixed height ; lowest in the entire arrangement.   Insert in *kenzan* behind the main *Tai* branch, extending to the right.—See diagram on page 206.

TOME GROUP :—Cut main branch $\frac{1}{2}$ the height of *Shin* and insert in *kenzan* behind and to the right of *Shin*.

SHO-FU-RYU KANSUI-IKE MORIBANA
Water-Viewing Arrangement
Gyakugatte or Left Hand Arrangement.

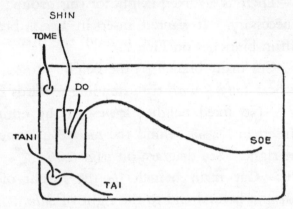

Showing positions of *kenzan* and main branches.

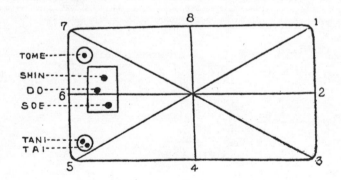

Showing positions of bases of main branches.

Order of Insertion

Cut lengths as for *Hongatte.*

SOE GROUP :—Insert in *kenzan* below Line 6 with tip extending over Line 3.

208

SHIN GROUP:—Insert in rear of *kenzan* above Line 6, standing upright with tip of branch over its base.

DO GROUP:—Sometimes not necessary; if wanted insert in *kenzan* between *Shin* and *Soe* main branches on Line 6.

TAI GROUP:—Insert in *kenzan* near Line 5, with tip extending towards Line 4.

TANI GROUP:—Insert in *kenzan* behind the main *Tai* branch extending outward to the left.

TOME GROUP:—Insert in *kenzan* behind and to the right of *Shin*.

MORIBANA

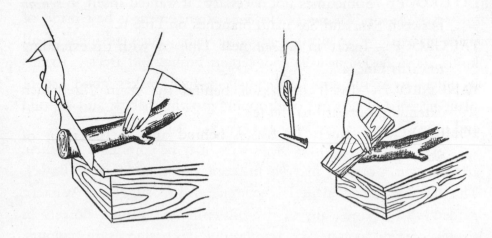

To arrange pine or other heavy tree branches : determine the angle at which the branch is to stand, and its proper length. Saw branch at required angle and nail a piece of wood to it, about 1/3 of the way from the end of the board.

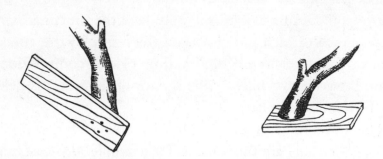

Use board in proportion to the size of your branch, and be careful that the length of the board is parallel with the branch, so that the longest end of the board is under the branch and resists the upward pull of the branch on the shorter end.

NAKA-MIZU KANSUI-IKE MORIBANA

A *Naka-mizu Kansui-ike Moribana* arrangement is best made of plant material of an upright-growing habit, such as lilies of all kinds, most garden flowers and certain bushes and trees. In this it differs from the simple *Kansui-ike* which makes good use of plant material of flowing or drooping growing habits, and of odd and unusual-shaped tree branches.

Any number of kinds of flowers may be combined for these arrangements ; or they may be made of only one kind of flower. This form of arrangement is recommended to suggest a Western garden with a pond ; any of the old-fashioned garden flowers in shades of one colour, or contrasting or harmonising colours, arranged in this way will bring the garden into your home and be a thing of joy.

Care must be taken to keep the two groups, *Shuza* and *Fukuza*, well separated ; at least half of the surface of the water should be left exposed and clear of flowers. The highest branch of each group should be toward the outside of the container with the shortest branch of each group toward the centre of the container ; this shows the water in a natural hollow of the composition as if a stream between two hills. The surface of the water is definitely a part of the desired effect.

The measurements of branches or flowers for a *Naka-Mizu Kansui-ike Moribana* are the same as for a simple *Moribana*, and the order of insertion is the same for both these arrangements.

MAE NO NAKA-MIZU KANSUI-IKE MORIBANA

Divided Water-Viewing Arrangement

Hongatte or Larger Arrangement to the Right-front.

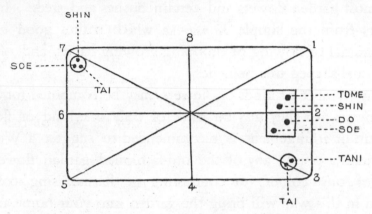

Showing positions of *kenzan* and bases of main branches.

SHUZA or LARGER GROUP

SHIN GROUP:—Cut main branch $1\frac{1}{2}$ to 2 times the width of the container and insert in *kenzan* above Line 2 with tip of branch above its base.   Add branches in back of and in front of this main branch as necessary.

SOE GROUP:—Cut length $\frac{2}{3}$ of *Shin* and insert in *kenzan* in front and to the left of *Shin*.   Add branches in front of and in back of as necessary.

DO GROUP:—Sometimes not necessary; if wanted insert in *kenzan* between *Shin* and *Soe*.

TAI GROUP:—Cut length $\frac{1}{3}$ of *Shin* and insert in *kenzan* on Line 3 between the *Soe* branch and the corner of the container. Add branches as necessary, keeping shape triangular.

212

TANI GROUP:—No fixed length—lowest part of the entire composition.   Insert in *kenzan* behind and to the right of *Tai*.

TOME GROUP:—Cut length half the height of *Shin* and insert in *kenzan* behind and to the right of *Shin*.   Add branches as necessary in front of this branch, but keep group scant.

FUKUZA or SMALLER GROUP

Construct a very simple *Shin, Soe, Tai* arrangement on Line 7, well in the rear corner of the container.   The *Tai* of this group should point towards the *Tai* of the larger group.   The *Shin* of this group should be about ³/₅ the length of the *Shin* of the larger group.

MAE NO NAKA-MIZU KANSUI-IKE MORIBANA
Divided Water-Viewing Arrangement
Gyakugatte or Larger Arrangement to the Left-front.

Showing positions of *kenzan* and bases of main branches.

SHUZA or LARGER GROUP

SHIN GROUP :—Cut main branch $1\frac{1}{2}$ to 2 times the width of the container and insert in *kenzan* above Line 6 with tip of branch above its base.   Add branches in back of and in front of this branch as necessary.

SOE GROUP :—Cut length $\frac{2}{3}$ of *Shin* and insert in *kenzan* in front and to the right of *Shin*.   Add branches in front of and in back of this branch as necessary.

DO GROUP :—Sometimes not necessary ; if wanted, insert in *kenzan* between *Shin* and *Soe*.

TAI GROUP :—Cut length $\frac{1}{3}$ of *Shin* and insert *kenzan* on Line 5. Add branches as necessary, keeping the shape triangular.

TANI GROUP :—No fixed length—shortest in the arrangement.

214

Insert in *kenzan* behind and to the left of *Tai*.

TOME GROUP :—Cut length half the length of *Shin* and insert in *kenzan* behind and to the left of *Shin*. Add branches in front of this branch as necessary, but keep group scant.

FUKUZA or SMALLER GROUP

Construct a simple *Shin*, *Soe*, *Tai* arrangement with *Tai* pointing towards the *Tai* of the larger group. Cut *Shin* $^3/_5$ the length of the *Shin* of the larger group. Insert in *kenzan* on Line 1.

215

OKU NO NAKA-MIZU KANSUI-IKE MORIBANA

Divided Water-Viewing Arrangement

Hongatte or Larger Arrangement to the Right-Rear.

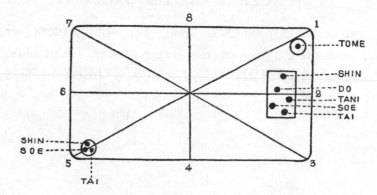

Showing positions of *kenzan* and bases of main branches.

SHUZA or LARGER GROUP

SHIN GROUP:—Cut main branch equal to $1\frac{1}{2}$ to 2 times the width of the container and insert in rear of *kenzan* upright with tip of branch over its base.   Add branches in front of and back of this branch as necessary.

SOE GROUP:—Cut main branch $\frac{2}{3}$ the length of *Shin* and insert in *kenzan* in front and to the left of *Shin* below Line 2. Add branches in front of and in back of this branch as necessary.

TAI GROUP:—Cut main branch $\frac{1}{3}$ of *Shin* and insert in *kenzan* in front and to the right of *Shin*, near Line 3.   Add branches as necessary between this branch and the *Shin* group.

TANI GROUP:—No fixed length—lowest branch of the arrangement.   Insert in *kenzan* behind and to the right of *Tai* about on Line 2.

TOME GROUP :—Cut main branch $1/2$ the length of *Shin*, and insert in *kenzan* behind and to the right of *Shin* about on Line 1.   Add branches in front of this branch as necessary but keep group scant.

FUKUZA or SMALLER GROUP

Construct a simple *Shin*, *Soe*, *Tai* arrangement on Line 5. Cut *Shin* equal to $3/5$ the height of the *Shin* of the larger group. See that the *Tai* of this group points towards the *Tai* of the larger group.

OKU NO NAKA-MIZU KANSUI-IKE MORIBANA

Divided Water-Viewing Arrangement

Gyakugatte or Larger Arrangement to the Left-Rear.

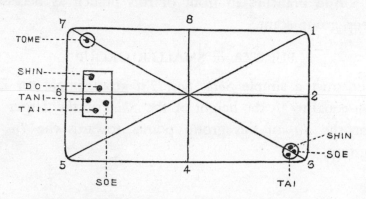

Showing positions of *kenzan* and bases or main branches.

SHUZA or LARGER GROUP

SHIN GROUP :—Cut main branch 1½ to 2 times the width of the container and insert in rear of *kenzan* upright with tip of branch over its base. Add branches in back of and in front of this branch as necessary.

SOE GROUP :—Cut main branch equal to ⅔ the length of the *Shin* branch and insert in *kenzan* in front and to the right of *Shin*. Add branches in back of and in front of this branch as necessary.

TAI GROUP :—Cut main branch ⅓ the length of *Shin* and insert in *kenzan* in front and to the left of *Shin*, near Line 6. Add branches between this branch and the *Shin* group as necessary.

TANI GROUP :—There is no fixed height for this group, it is the lowest of the entire arrangement. Insert in *kenzan* behind and to the left of *Tai*.

TOME GROUP :—Cut main branch ¹/₂ the height of *Shin* branch, and insert in *kenzan* behind and to the left of *Shin*, about on Line 7. Add necessary branches in front of this main branch but keep the entire group scant.

FUKUZA or SMALLER GROUP

Construct a simple *Shin, Soe, Tai* arrangement on Line 3 with *Shin* ³/₅ the height of the *Shin* of the larger group. The *Tai* branch of this group should point towards the *Tai* branch of the larger group.

SHO·FU·RYU MORIBANA

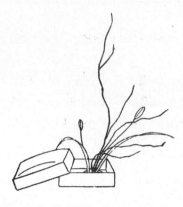

Gyakugatte or Left Hand Arrangement.

A thing of beauty and a moral lesson. Many of the Japanese flower arrangements suggest some episode in Japan's long history. This refers to the story of Ota Dokan, a famous warrior, who, in the middle of the fifteenth century, built the first castle in what is to-day the great city of Tokyo. However, this composition does not commemorate the founding of the city, but refers to a more romantic event in his life.

One day, while he was hunting in the mountains he was overtaken by a storm and stopped at a lowly hut to ask the loan of a rain coat. A young girl, obviously of gentle birth despite her humble surroundings, listened to his request; but instead of complying plucked a flower from the bush at the door and gave it to him, at the same time quoting the words of an old Japanese poem :—

> *" Nana e yae hana wa sake domo Yamabuki no*
> *mino hitotsu dani naki zo kanashiki."*

This poem explains that the flower she gave him bore no seed; but another interpretation could also mean that while many flowers grew in her garden she had no rain coat to lend him.

Ota Dokan was angry; but his followers, better educated than he, explained the allusion to him. Chagrined at being put to shame by a mere girl, he applied himself to the study of the classics and in after life became famous for his learning.

Both the blossom of the vine-like Jews mallow and the day lily are yellow, while the porcelain box in which they are arranged repeats that colour in the wheel pattern on a dark purple ground.

TO ARRANGE

SHIN GROUP :—Select a slender branch of the mallow; leave on all small branches; cut about twice the width of the table. Bend to the shape of the *Shin* branch in an *Ike-no-bo* arrangement. Place *kenzan* well to the front at the right-hand corner of the box. Insert *Shin* branch in *kenzan* on Line 2. Take care that the branch is balanced, with the extreme tip over its base.

SOE GROUP :—Cut equal to half of *Shin*;—bend to the shape of an *Ike-no-bo Soe*. Insert in *kenzan* on Line 3. Now select a day lily with a long leaf and insert just behind the second branch;—make the curve of the leaf conform to the curve of the branch by gently bending it with the fingers.

TANI GROUP :—Select a short branch of the mallow, one with profuse leaves, and insert in *kenzan* on Line 4 leaning towards you.

TAI GROUP :—Insert day lily on Line 5; bend leaf in graceful curve to balance the curves of *Shin* and *Soe*. Now add second day lily cut shorter than *Tai* lily; insert just behind that lily and lean it the least bit to the left. If necessary add short leaves of the day lily, enough to hide the *kenzan*.

NOTE :—The table or stand on which the arrangement is displayed is considered part of the composition.

220

SHO-FU-RYU MORIBANA

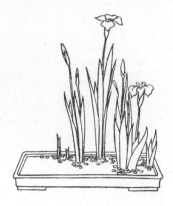

Hongatte Gyodo or Right Hand "Fish-path" Arrangement.

A charming arrangement of purple irises. The Japanese never crowd their flowers; a very common iris arrangement is of but three blossoms and their leaves. This is a Summer composition and suggests vividly a bed of irises on a hot day.

In arranging irises, great care must be taken with the leaves. Note that the leaves grow naturally two by two with points opposing.

SHIN GROUP:—Select tall purple iris, cut about twice the width of the container, or use as long as possible. Insert upright in *kenzan* on Line 1, well to the rear of the container. Now insert three sets of opposing leaves in front of this flower and two sets to the rear; cut each set a different length and arrange to look as if growing from one root.

SOE GROUP:—Select half-open iris; cut ¾ the height of *Shin*. Insert in *kenzan* on Line 7 leaning slightly to the left and forward. Now cut tight bud ⅔ the length of this flower and insert in *kenzan* a little to the front and to the right of same. Follow angle of first flower.

Add three sets of opposing leaves in front and two sets of opposing leaves in back of these two flowers, to appear as if growing from one root.

TOME GROUP:—Cut tight bud half the length of *Shin* and insert in *kenzan* on Line 2; surround this bud with sets of opposing leaves, two in front, one in back to simulate a growing plant.

TAI GROUP:—Select full-blown flower about ⅓ the length of *Shin*, and insert in *kenzan* between Lines 3 and 4. This group differs from the other groups in that one set of the opposing leaves is made up of three leaves. Insert this three-leaf group and two opposing leaf groups in front of the *Tai* flower; add two sets of opposing leaves in back.

TANI GROUP:—Leaves only—half the height of *Tai* flower—insert three sets of opposing leaves on Line 2.

NOTE:—Cover *kenzan* with pebbles and on the left insert a couple of sets of leaves cut very short. These can be made to stand upright in the pebbles and represent new plants shooting up out of the water. Each group of flowers and leaves should appear to be a growing plant.

This arrangement is called a "Fish-path" arrangement because of the open spaces at the base of the flowers through which fish can swim.

222

SHO-FU-RYU MORIBANA

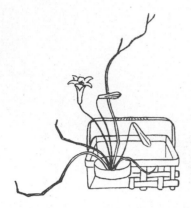

Hongatte or Right Hand Arrangement.

This arrangement is composed of half a dozen sprays of wild strawberry and a couple of Easter lilies. The fresh new green of the vine and the clear whiteness of the lilies arranged in a basket of natural coloured bamboo bring into the house a breath of Spring and express joy over release from the cold of Winter.

TO ARRANGE

SHIN GROUP :—Select a crescent-shaped branch of the wild strawberry if possible—it may be necessary to bend one into the desired shape. Cut once and a half the width of the basket and insert in *kenzan* so that the tip falls over the middle of the basket. Place *kenzan* in front of the handle; no part of the arrangement goes behind the handle and care must be taken that no part touches it.

SHIN MAE :—Now insert a second branch shorter than the first, conforming to the curve of the *Shin* branch.

MIKOSHI :—Insert a third branch shorter than the second to the left of the *Shin* branch, but leaning away from it, about over Line 6. This makes the *Shin* group. In itself it should be a complete group of pleasing proportion. (Note that this simple grouping conforms to the *Shin-Soe-Tai* of all Japanese arrangements).

SOE GROUP :—Select a curved branch with a tip curving vigorously upwards. Never allow the tip of any branch to droop downwards—that expresses weakness, and a Japanese arrangement always expresses growth and strength.

Insert this branch in the *kenzan* on Line 5. The length of this branch should be ⅔ that of the *Shin* branch.

DO GROUP :—Use full-blown lily. Insert in *kenzan* between *Shin* and *Soe* following the line of the *Shin* branch and at a harmonious height with relation to both *Shin* and *Soe*.

TANI GROUP :—Use a short piece of the wild strawberry with plenty of leaves. Insert in *kenzan* on Line 4. This branch should fill in the arrangement and bind into unity the various parts.

TAI GROUP :—Select slender rather straight branch of the wild strawberry; cut ⅓ the length of *Shin* and insert in *kenzan* on Line 3, extending well outside the basket and pointing off to the right. Now insert a lily bud just behind the *Tai* branch.

NOTE :—The tip of the three main branches—*Shin-Soe-Tai*—form a triangle and the colours of the lily and lily-buds form one in colour. The ends of the branches are inserted close together in the *kenzan* following the same line for three or four inches as though one growing plant. In arranging flowers in a basket the Japanese always avoid a crowded look and leave the handle clear so that the basket can actually be carried by it. This wild strawberry is a bush; therefore suggest that, by using short branches of it to hide *kenzan;* do not use moss.

224

SHO-FU-RYU MORIBANA

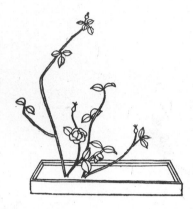

Gyakugatte Kansui Ike or Left Hand Arrangement.

Roses in a long narrow blue-green container.

Place *kenzan* against front edge of container about one quarter of the way from the left front corner. Long sprays of rose leaves add interest to an otherwise commonplace arrangement of pink roses.

TO ARRANGE

SOE GROUP :—Select a long slender spray of roses with bud at tip and cut 1½ times the length of the container. Trim off most of the leaves and all twigs to show line of stem. Insert in *kenzan* on Line 6 leaning the least bit to the left.

SHIN GROUP :—Straight spray with bud at the tip; cut ½ the length of *Soe*. Insert on Line 8 upright with tip over its base.

DO GROUP :—Use full-blown rose, half the length of *Shin*. Line 5.

TAI GROUP :—Use strong-looking bud; cut ⅔ the length of *Shin*. Insert in *kenzan* leaning forward over Line 3.

TANI GROUP :—Half-open bud on Line 4.

NOTE :—Hide *kenzan* with rose leaves ; do not use moss.

226

SHO-FU-RYU MORIBANA

Hongatte or Right Hand Arrangement.

An interesting composition of dragon willow and Easter lilies, very modern in feeling yet conforming to age-old standards. The vase used is a soft sage-green crackle ware of unusual shape.

TO ARRANGE

SOE GROUP :—This arrangement was designed to make use of a naturally twisted branch of the dragon willow ; therefore it is used quite long to accentuate the shape. Insert in *kenzan* leaning slightly to the left on Line 6.

SHIN GROUP :—Cut branch of the dragon willow about half the height of *Soe*. Insert upright on Line 7.

DO GROUP :—Use stalk of Easter lily, with open flower ; cut slightly shorter than *Shin;* insert in front of *Shin* at an angle to conform with *Soe*—about on Line 5.

TAI GROUP :—Insert Easter lily bud leaning forward over Line 3.

NOTE :—Keep the bases of the willow branches together—also the lily stems—the completed arrangement is to suggest a lily plant growing naturally at the foot of a willow tree.

SHO-FU-RYU MORIBANA

Hongatte Futa-Kabu or Right Hand Divided Root Arrangement.

An unusual combination of plant materials but one of uncommon beauty. The vivid colours of the orange lily and rosy cyclamen are softened and harmonised by the grey-green of the acacia sprays. The beauty of the strong up-springing lines of the arrangement is typically Japanese. Note that the *Shin* and *Soe* groups' proportions are the reverse of the usual *Morihana* rules; *Soe* is the tallest branch and *Shin* ⅔ of it. This produces an agreeable variation and avoids a monotonous step-arrangement.

SHUZA, OR LARGER GROUP

SOE GROUP:—Use spray of acacia and cut 1½ the diameter of the container. Insert in *kenzan* on Line 5.

SHIN GROUP:—Cut spray of acacia ⅔ the height of *Soe* and insert in *kenzan* on Line 7.

DO GROUP:—Insert lily bloom between *Shin* and *Soe* to bring the two into unity.

TANI GROUP:—Use lily—shorter than the *Do* lily. Insert in *kenzan* between Lines 4 and 5.

TAI GROUP:—Cut spray of acacia ⅓ the height of *Soe* and insert in *kenzan* on Line 4.

FUKUZA, OR SMALLER GROUP

Make a very simple *Shin-Soe-Tai* arrangement of the cyclamen, with the *Tai* pointing towards the *Tai* of the *Shuza* group. Use flowers as long as possible; do not cut; and keep leaves low to suggest the natural growing habit of this plant.

SHO-FU-RYU MORIBANA

Hongatte Shikisai or Right Hand Arrangement for Colour.

An arrangement for joy of colour, friendly and bright in its simple white bowl on a bamboo mat. Consists of three branches of hydrangea, a couple of orange lilies and a spray of yellow pink chrysanthemums.

TO ARRANGE

SHIN GROUP :—Select a pretty branch of hydrangea, one without a flower. Cut once and a half the width of the bowl. Insert in *kenzan* a little to the left of the middle of the bowl on Line 6.

SOE GROUP :—Use freshest-looking medium-sized hydrangea flower; in the picture two on one stem are considered as one. Cut ⅔ length of *Shin*.
Insert in *kenzan* leaning a little to the left and forward over Line 5.

DO GROUP :—Largest hydrangea flower—this should be a little higher than the *Soe*, but shorter than the *Shin* branch. Insert in front of *Shin*.

TANI GROUP :—Orange lily, full blown. Cut about 6″ long. Insert in *kenzan* leaning forward at Line 4.

TAI GROUP :—Half-opened lily cut ⅛ the length of *Shin*. Insert in *kenzan* leaning to the right at Line 3. Now add lily bud nearer the *Shin* branch to form triangle with the two other lily blossoms.

TOME GROUP :—Use chrysanthemum bud. Cut ½ length of *Shin*. Insert in *kenzan* on Line 8; lean slightly forward. Add a full-blown chrysanthemum just a little shorter than the bud, in front of it and behind the *Tani* lily, and another much shorter in front of these two.

NOTE :—In this composition, colour rather than line is stressed. Hide *kenzan* with leaves of hydrangea.

SHO-FU-RYU MORIBANA

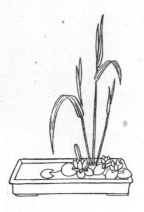

Hongatte Kansui Ike or Right Hand Water-viewing Arrangement.

A composition of ribbon grass and water lilies in a white container—an informal arrangement for a hot day.

TO ARRANGE

SHIN GROUP :—Cut stalk of ribbon grass twice the width of the container. Insert in *kenzan* on Line 1; coax leaves to follow line of main stalk; they must not branch out at all angles; see that the tips of all leaves point straight up.

SOE GROUP :—Select a stalk with one large strong leaf (or one single strong leaf) and gently bend it into shape. Insert in *kenzan* in front of *Shin* with tip drooping towards the left front corner of the container, over Line 5.

DO GROUP :—Stalk of ribbon grass; cut so that extreme tip reaches about half the height of the *Shin*. This should have a large strong leaf drooping to the front. Insert in *kenzan* in front of *Shin*. Note that the *Shin* group now is a slender straight arrangement, having a *Shin-Soe-Tai* on its own. However, when arranging two water plants together the Japanese consider the composition as a whole and the water lilies are included with the taller grasses in each main group; though the stem roots of each are kept together in the *kenzan* as if growing naturally. The lily leaves and blossoms must appear to be floating on the surface of the water and must be grouped naturally as though growing.

Now cut the stems of the three largest lily leaves to about one inch. Insert in *kenzan* grouped naturally around a full-blown water lily on Line 6. Take a small long-stemmed leaf and insert stem in *kenzan* under lily group with its leaf extending out toward the left front corner of the container. Just in the rear of the flower in this group insert a tight rolled leaf bud, with the fold of the leaf facing the front.

TOMI GROUP :—Form group of small open water lily with three medium-sized leaves; insert in Line 2.

TAI GROUP :—Use largest water lily, three large leaves and two smaller ones. Form natural group, as though growing.

NOTE :—Care should be taken that the *kenzan* are properly covered and that the water-lily blossoms do not stick up out of the water too far. Keep the water clean looking—the whole effect is spoiled by hot-looking stagnant water.

SHO-FU-RYU MORIBANA

Hongatte Kansui Ike or Right Hand Water-viewing Arrangement.

The arrangement of a single calla lily and its leaves with but two slender reeds, simple as it is, suggests the freedom of a vast moor.

Care must be taken with the background for this composition, as a confused or highly coloured one would spoil the effect.

Such arrangements as this are very effective if placed before a mirror.

TO ARRANGE

SHIN GROUP :—Cut stem of the calla lily about twice the width of the container, or as long as the flower permits. Insert in *kenzan* on Line 2, upright with flower facing you. Add one leaf at rear of flower, with tip pointing to the left.

SOE GROUP :—Cut a large strong leaf ⅔ the height of *Shin;* carefully bend leaf into gentle curve (suggestive of the *Soe* branch of an *Ike-no-bo* arrangement). Insert in *kenzan* pointing over Line 5.

DO GROUP :—Insert strong little leaf upright in front of *Shin* with tip pointing towards you, Line 5.

TANI GROUP :—Now insert small leaf about 6″ high, pointing forward, to hide stems as much as possible.

TAI GROUP :—Cut leaf about half the length of the *Shin* flower and insert at an angle so that the apparent height of this leaf is ⅓ the height of the *Shin* leaf; tip of leaf over Line 3. Insert two tall reeds, one tall one upright in *kenzan* just in front of *Shin* ; this should be taller than the *Shin* flower. Insert second reed behind *Tai* in the *kenzan*—upright—but bend (or break) tip sharply at a point about the same distance below the flower as the tip of the first reed is above the flower.

NOTE :—Carefully cover *kenzan* with small pebbles ; do not pile pebbles around base of arrangement ; but spread out as if washed into that shape by waves.

The leaves should be arranged around the flower stem at the centre as though actually growing. The broken reed is used for its suggestion of naturalness as well as to add variety to the line of the composition.

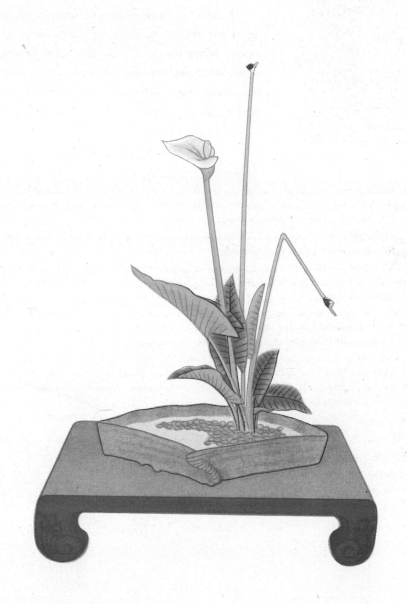

SHO-FU-RYU MORIBANA

Hongatte Kansui Ike or Right Hand Water-viewing Arrangement.

A Summer arrangement of lotus blossoms in white oblong container on black lacquered wood adjustable base. In this composition, seed-pod, flower and bud are used, representing the three stages of human life—past, present and future.

TO ARRANGE

SHIN GROUP:—Use tight bud; cut length twice the width of the container. Insert in *kenzan* so that the bud is balanced on its long slender stem, on Line 2. Add half-opened leaf bud a little shorter than *Shin;* face leaf to front; insert to rear and right of *Shin*.

MIKOSHI:—Cut seed-pod a little shorter than *Shin*. Insert a little to the front and left of *Shin*—at an angle conforming to that of *Shin*.

DO GROUP:—Use large half-open leaf cut about half the length of *Shin*. Insert in front of *Shin* on Line 3. Add open blossom.

SOE GROUP:—Select tight rolled leaf bud. Cut ⅔ the length of *Shin*. Insert in second *kenzan* to the left of the front, leaning slightly to the left. Now add open leaf, medium size, about half the length of *Soe*. Insert half-open flower bud to the rear of *Soe*—a little shorter than the other two *Soe* stems.

TAI GROUP:—In third *kenzan*, in front of first, insert a large leaf leaning well to the front over Line 3 with stem not more than three inches. Now insert tight-rolled leaf bud just behind the *Tai* leaf as though it were a new growth shooting up at the base of the *Shin* group.

NOTE:—Hide *kenzan* with small leaves arranged as though floating on the surface of the water, taking care that they appear to be growing naturally from a definite root.

SHO-FU-RYU MORIBANA

Gyakugatte Kansui Ike or Left Hand Water-viewing Arrangement.

A delightful arrangement, reminiscent of a picnic on the edge of a lake : two beautiful gnarled branches of pine with flowers as though growing naturally. The addition of a water-worn stone and the rough surface of the wooden container heighten the effect of naturalness.

TO ARRANGE

SHIN and SOE GROUPS :—Advantage is taken of the natural shape of these branches, but their proportion to the container must be considered. *Shin* is about 1½ times the width of the container, *Soe* about the length of the diagonal of same. Place *Shin* on Line 7 at an angle as in illustration ; add *Soe* on Line 3 to conform with *Shin*. The natural growth of the pine needles determines the angle at which these branches are to be fixed. Cut off any small twigs that detract from the effect of an upward-reaching growth. Face the best side of the branch towards you, not to the rear of the arrangement. Remember that in Japanese flower arrangements your position is south with relation to the arrangement and plants grow naturally towards the south.

DO GROUP :—Do not make this heavy enough to hide the large branches ; the idea is to suggest growing trees—use only two or three small pinks with their buds.

TAI GROUP :—Now insert a rather small bunchy group of the yellow chrysanthemums. Keep flowers low and scant to suggest vegetation at the foot of a tree.

NOTE :—The stones serve two purposes ; they are part of the composition but also serve to balance the heavy branches upright.

SHO-FU-RYU MORIBANA

Gyakugatte Kansui Ike or Left Hand Water-viewing Arrangement.

The contrast between the sturdy fruit-bearing pomegranate and the dainty garden pinks is delightful and suggests the comforting shade of an old orchard on a Summer day. The arrangement pictured has used the leaves of a wild orchid to give further lightness and delicacy.

TO ARRANGE

SHIN GROUP :—Select a rather straight slender branch with fruit at the tip if possible. Cut once and a half the width of the container. Insert in *kenzan* on Line 6, just the least bit to the left of the centre of the container.

MIKOSHI :—Cut a more sturdy branch bearing fruit a little shorter than the *Shin* and insert in *kenzan* a little to the rear and to the left of *Shin*.

SOE GROUP :—For this arrangement an old dead branch of the pomegranate tree has been used. Its shape is interesting and it gives an appearance of age and strength to the composition. Now almost cover the bareness of this branch by full-leaved branches inserted in front and to the rear. Do not make the branches conform too closely in shape but suggest new shoots growing from an old trunk as in the picture.

DO GROUP :—Use full-leaved heavily fruited branch. Cut to height to bring entire composition down and unite the *Shin* and *Soe* branches.

TANI GROUP :—Now insert a group of the orchid leaves and a spray of the garden pinks in front of the *Do* branch, extending out to Line 4.

TAI GROUP :—Cut a branch of the pomegranate ⅓ the length of *Shin*,—this should have leaves only and its tip should reach upwards (not droop). Insert in *kenzan* on Line 5 and extend outward over the edge of the container. Soften this part of the arrangement with a spray of garden pinks.

TOME GROUP :—Insert a tall spray of the garden pink, about half the height of the *Shin* branch, a little to the left and rear of *Shin*, on Line 7.

NOTE :—When arranging fruit-bearing branches and flowers, the fruit is always placed at the top with the flowers in the lower part of the composition.

Branches of large trees are always arranged showing line of stem to suggest trunk of tree. Do not allow small short branches of the pomegranate at the base of the larger stronger branches; if you wish to soften the effect of the composition add flowers or leaves that naturally grow at the foot of a tree.

242

SHO-FU-RYU MORIBANA

Hongatte Kansui Ike or Right Hand Water-viewing Arrangement.

An arrangement of bitter sweet and Easter lilies in a Chinese blue container. A very simple but pleasing composition for late Summer.

TO ARRANGE

SOE GROUP :—Select a long slender branch of the bitter sweet, one with an interesting tip; strip off most of the berries and small leaves leaving only those on the tip. Cut equal to once and a half the diameter of the container. Insert in *kenzan* on Line 4 with tip falling over Line 7.

SHIN GROUP :—Use a branch heavy with berries; cut about half the length of *Soe*. Insert in *kenzan* so that tip falls over Line 1.

MIKOSHI :—Cut half-open Easter lily ⅔ the length of *Shin*, insert in *kenzan* on Line 1, lean slightly away from *Shin*, about over Line 8, to the left.

DO GROUP :—Use full-blown Easter lily. Insert on Line 8 at an angle to conform with *Soe*, to the right of that branch and leaning forward.

TAI GROUP :—In the arrangement illustrated this is the most interesting branch of the whole composition; one fork serves as *Tome* on Line 2 while the tip of the other fork falls over Line 4. Now add lily bud at an angle to agree with *Tai*, tip to fall over Line 5.

NOTE :—The stems of the berries should be inserted in the *kenzan* as close together as possible to suggest one growing plant—so also the lilies.

SHO-FU-RYU MORIBANA

Hongatte or Right Hand Arrangement.

An autumn arrangement of cosmos and millet stalks in a woven bamboo basket, typically Japanese in feeling; the fresh vital growth of the cosmos contrasted with the sereness of the millet is delightfully suggestive of the season. The flowers are arranged in a small porcelain container placed in one corner of the basket.

This arrangement is interesting in that the *Shin* and *Soe* branches have changed proportions but not positions.

TO ARRANGE

SOE GROUP :—Cut a stalk of the millet about twice the width of the basket and insert in *kenzan* in the *Soe* position upright on Line 7.

SHIN GROUP :—Use spray of cosmos about half the height of *Soe*.

DO GROUP :—Cosmos, only about half the length of the first spray.

TAI GROUP :—Stalk of millet; cut ⅔ the length of *Soe*, insert in *kenzan* leaning slightly forward over Line 4, break stalk about ⅓ the distance from tip to base.

246

SHO-FU-KYU MORIBANA

Hongatte Kansui Ike or Right Hand Water-viewing Arrangement.

This arrangement illustrates the Japanese love of line and simple uncrowded compositions. In Japan the camellia blooms almost the whole year round, and it is a very favourite flower with lovers of *Ike-bana ;*—its glossy leaves and brilliant waxy flowers lend themselves to many different treatments. Here pink camellia blossoms are arranged in a blue-green flat oval container.

TO ARRANGE

SHIN GROUP :—Select a fairly straight branch and cut about twice the diameter of the container. Cut off flowers and leaves so as to expose the line of the stem. Insert in *kenzan* on Line 1 upright, with its tip over its base.

MIKOSHI :—In this arrangement the flower acts as *Mikoshi.* If lacking, add small branch with flower at tip. Follow as closely as possible the illustration (no two branches are ever alike) but keep same general arrangement of line.

SOE GROUP :—Select a branch with an interesting tip curving upward. Be careful never to allow the tip of any main branch to droop. In this composition the upward-turning tip adds great strength as well as beauty of line to the arrangement. Strip off all leaves and flowers except just at the tip and thin those out so that the buds are exposed. Insert in *kenzan* on Line 2—tip falling over Line 5.

DO GROUP :—Select small slender branch with bud at tip ; strip off all leaves and flowers that confuse the line of the branch. Insert in *kenzan* in front of *Shin,* leaning forward over Line 5.

TANI GROUP :—Full-blown blossom and full leaves. Insert in *kenzan* between Lines 2 and 3, upright.

TAI GROUP :—Select full-leaved branch with bud at tip ; cut ½ of *Shin.* Insert in *kenzan* between Lines 3 and 4, leaning well forward. Be sure that the bud faces upward, do not allow to droop.

TOME GROUP :—Cut branch of camellia about ½ height of *Shin ;* insert a little to the rear and to the right of *Shin* on Line 1.

Now make three groups of wild orchid leaves of different lengths and insert one each under the *Tome, Tani* and *Tai* branches to soften and tie the composition together.

NOTE :—The roots of the camellia branches should be together in the *kenzan* to suggest a tree.

The camellia in Japan is a tree, therefore do not add small branches of it at the base of the larger stronger branches ; this not only confuses the line but suggests a bush rather than a tree. To soften the arrangement use a plant that grows naturally at the foot of a tree—in this case the orchid.

SHO-FU-RYU MORIBANA

Gyakugatte Oku no Naka-mizu Kansui Ike or Left Hand Arrangement.

An attractive arrangement of Oregon grape and common yellow daisies. The leaves of the wild orchid have been added for contrast and to soften the composition. For this arrangement the larger group, or *Shuza*, is placed in the rear of the dish and the smaller group, *Fukuza*, in the front.

Use two *kenzan*; place the larger one between Lines 6 and 7 and the smaller one between Lines 2 and 3.

Note that while this arrangement is made up of two separate and distinct groups, each triangular in shape and complete in itself, the composition as a whole is triangular.

TO ARRANGE

SHUZA

SOE GROUP :—Select long strong branch of the Oregon grape and cut it once and a half the length of the container. Insert in *kenzan* about on Line 6.

SHIN GROUP :—Cut branch of the Oregon grape ⅔ the height of the *Soe* branch and insert in *kenzan* about on Line 7.

DO GROUP :—Branch of Oregon grape; insert in *kenzan* between *Soe* and *Shin*.

TAI GROUP :—Use yellow daisy but make this group quite scant and point forward on Line 5.

TANI GROUP :—Add yellow daisies to soften the composition and hide *kenzan*. Do not make too full arrangement because while this *Shuza* group is complete in itself with *Shin*, *Soe*, *Tai*, etc., actually it is the *Shin* and *Soe* groups of the entire arrangement.

TOME GROUP :—Add spray of wild orchid leaves behind *Shin*—to balance this part of the arrangement and bring the eyes to rest.

FUKUZA

Use only Oregon grape and club moss. Again the *Soe* branch is longer than the *Shin* branch. In this smaller group the moss is to be considered as the *Tai*.

Be careful to leave a good space between the two groups, the water is a part of the composition.

SHO-FU-RYU MORIBANA

Hongatte or Right Hand Arrangement.

A simple composition of white Chinese lilies in a red lacquer bowl, lovely in colour and fresh in feeling.

In arranging Chinese lilies the Japanese re-group the leaves and flowers so that the leaves follow closely the line of the stem of the flowers and do not overtop them. They never allow the leaves to droop and cross one another. Use one large *kenzan* in bottom of bowl.

TO ARRANGE

SHIN GROUP :—Use a long spray of lilies. Coax leaves to stay close and follow the line of the flower stem. Insert in *kenzan* on Line 7 halfway between edge and centre of bowl. Stand upright with flowers facing you.

MIKOSHI :—Select flower and leaf group slightly shorter than *Shin* and insert in *kenzan* a little to the rear and to the left of *Shin*.

SOE GROUP :—Select flower and leaf group about ⅔ the height of *Shin* and insert in *kenzan* on Line 5 ; lean slightly forward and to the left.

DO GROUP :—Flower and leaf group slightly longer than *Mikoshi*. Insert in front of *Shin* on Line 5.

TANI GROUP :—Insert quite short flower and leaf group in front of *Do* on Line 4.

TAI GROUP :—Use bud group only. Cut to ⅓ height of *Shin*, allowing one long strong leaf to extend to the right as illustrated. Insert in *kenzan* on Line 4 and in front of *Tani* with long leaf falling over Line 3.

TOME GROUP :—Flower and leaf group ½ height of *Shin*. Insert on Line 8 a little to the right and rear of *Shin*.

NOTE :—Be careful that leaves follow line of flower stems and do not cross. Only the *Tai* leaf has a gentle curve away from its flower.

252

SHO-FU-RYU MORIBANA

Hongatte or Right Hand Arrangement.

An arrangement of pine and roses before a wall-hanging showing the rising sun over peaceful ocean waves, a very typical composition and much liked by the Japanese. The basket is natural coloured and is one used by fishermen to hold the daily catch. The pine branch is of a species which grows on the seashore. This arrangement is considered most appropriate for occasions of rejoicing; it is a common New Year decoration.

TO ARRANGE

SOE GROUP:—Only one large pine branch is used for the arrangement illustrated. It has been trimmed and cleared of all small branches and needle clumps that would hide the shape of the moss-covered branches. The pine cones are carefully left on. If such a large branch is not available, two small ones may be used; then the *Soe* branch would be cut to a length equal to the height plus the width of the basket. Insert at an angle on Line 5.

SHIN GROUP:—Cut length equal to once and a half the height of the basket. Insert upright just behind the *Soe*.

TANI GROUP:—Use a rose—this should be about ⅓ the height of *Shin*. Insert in front of *Shin* extending forward and slightly to the right of Line 4.

TAI GROUP:—Use longest rose, this should be ½ of *Shin*. Insert front of *Shin* extending out forward at Line 3. Add third rose behind the first two, to make triangle in height and colour.

NOTE:—Now add wild orchid leaf-blades to soften the arrangement.

SHO-FU-RYU MORIBANA

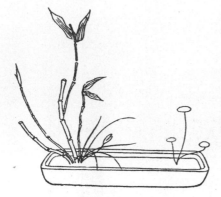

Gyakugatte Mae no Naka-mizu Kansui Ike or Left Hand Arrangement.

An arrangement suggesting a mountain stream in late Summer. Bamboo grass, wild orchids, brake-fern and small white chrysanthemums are shown arranged in a long brown pottery container. The plant material is simple, but the whole composition is most pleasing, revealing the unsuspected beauty in common plants.

This composition consists of two groups—each complete in itself, but mutually complementary.

TO ARRANGE

SHUZA, OR LARGER ARRANGEMENT

SHIN GROUP :—Select an interesting stalk of the bamboo grass and cut it twice the width of the container. Do not attempt to bend, as this plant naturally grows upright. Insert in *kenzan* on Line 6.

SOE GROUP :—This arrangement has made use of a crooked stalk of the bamboo grass whose curve approximates the desired *Soe* curve. Cut ⅔ the height of *Shin* and insert on Line 5.

USHIROZOE :—This *Soe* branch is a most interesting shape—the long slender off-shoots serve as both *Ushirozoe* and *Mikoshi*.

TAI GROUP :—Cut stalk of bamboo grass with pretty leaves ⅓ the height of *Shin*. Insert on Line 4 at an angle leaning well forward.

The roots of these groups, *Shin-Soe-Tai*, should be kept well together, as though a growing unit.

TOME GROUP :—Use tallest group of wild orchid leaves and insert behind and a little to the right of *Shin*.

TANI GROUP :—Cut one group of wild orchid leaves rather short and arrange about seed pod. Insert this at the rear of the *Tai* branch of bamboo grass.

Allow leaves of the wild orchid to fall naturally in all directions.

FUKUZA, OR SMALLER GROUP

SHIN GROUP :—Select rather sparse branches of the small white chrysanthemum, or cut away some of the full-blown blossoms to make a light dainty arrangement—too full would over-balance the main group. Cut branch ⁸/₁₀ the height of the *Shin* of the larger group. Insert in *kenzan* on Line 2.

SOE GROUP :—⅔ the height of *Shin*, insert on Line 3.

TAI GROUP :—⅓ the height of *Shin*, between Lines 3 and 4.

NOTE :—Now arrange brake-fern so as to hide *kenzan* and simulate the ground by the side of a mountain stream. Isolate the smaller group—it represents the vegetation on the other side of the stream; do not use fern but if necessary hide *kenzan* with chrysanthemum leaves.

SHO-FU-RYU MORIBANA

Hongatte Kansui Ike or Right Hand Arrangement.

A *Sho-chiku-bai* arrangement—always used for New Year's decoration because of its symbolism. Both the pine and the bamboo are evergreens, signifying unchangeableness—the pine further typifies strength—the bamboo uprightness of character. The plum is the first tree to flower in the Spring, its blossoms open even in the snow; to the Japanese it typifies perseverance in spite of adverse circumstances. Chrysanthemums are sometimes used to add a bit of colour and lightness to the composition. The chrysanthemum holds a high place in the estimation of the Japanese; it is considered suitable and appropriate for any occasion, no matter how formal. Where Europeans would use orchids or roses the Japanese use chrysanthemums.

The use of the bamboo is hedged round with many restrictions;—according to the rules of the *Ike-no-bo*, and *Sho-fu-ryu*, the stalks must be cut horizontally not obliquely,—an odd number, never an even number of joints must show in any arrangement, and for a formal arrangement the bamboo must be considered as a grass and be placed in the front of the arrangement. The arrangement illustrated is considered informal.

TO ARRANGE

SHIN GROUP :—Carefully select three stalks of bamboo, cut the tallest twice the width of the container, cut away all unnecessary leaf twigs, leaving one long enough to act as the *Shin ushiro* branch. Take care that the joints come at the desired position, with an odd number showing. Insert in *kenzan* on Line 1, halfway between centre and edge of container.

SOE GROUP :—Use length of bamboo shorter than *Shin*, with slender leaf branch for *Soe* branch.

   USHIROZOE :—A little to the left and rear of the *Soe* bamboo, insert on Line 1, bamboo and centre of container, a heavy moss-covered plum branch, add one or more flower-twigs at an angle conforming to the moss-covered branch—but not many, just enough to suggest a flowering tree.

DO GROUP :—Use length of bamboo shorter than *Soe*—the difference between *Shin* and *Soe*, and the difference between *Soe* and *Do* should be the same, and an odd number of joints should be visible.

TAI GROUP :—Use small red berries such as wintergreen berries, insert in a low bunchy group, between Lines 3 and 4.

TOME GROUP :—Use pine branch, insert on Line 1, between bamboo and edge of container, about half the height of *Shin*.

NOTE :—Now cover the *kenzan* and form a long natural-looking triangle with club moss to suggest a water-side scene.

Small white chrysanthemums or woods blossoms may be substituted for the berries.

SHO-FU-RYU MORIBANA

Hongatte Kansui Ike or Right Hand Water-viewing Arrangement.

This composition of moss-covered plum branches with their tiny pearl-like buds and soft pink roses in a black lacquered dish is one of unusual charm.

The plum flower is much loved by the Japanese because it blooms while the snow is yet on the ground, and it is used as a symbol of Japanese womanhood. In this arrangement the plum branches suggest the strength and the roses the beauty of the spirit of Japanese womanhood, strong in the blasts of adversity but gracious and yielding in the shelter of the family.

TO ARRANGE

SOE GROUP :—Select a sturdy moss-covered branch of the plum, of an interesting shape if possible, with a blossoming tip shooting upwards—never allow the tip of any main branch to droop listlessly. Trim off all small branches on the under side of this branch. It represents that very common sight—an old tree forced over by the wind and weather, yet gallantly sending out new growth. Insert in *kenzan* so that the tip will fall over Line 5.

SHIN GROUP :—Usually this branch is cut about twice the diameter of the container but to give the feeling of vigour we will lengthen it. Select a branch strong enough looking to harmonise with the *Soe* branch as in the illustration. Insert in *kenzan* between Lines 1 and 2, balanced with its tip over its base.

 MIKOSHI :—Select a branch with many blossoms, cut a little shorter than *Shin*, and insert in *kenzan* between *Shin* and *Soe*. Incline just a bit to conform with the *Soe* branch. Now add another branch with not too many blossoms to the right and rear of *Shin;*—take care that this is a different height from any other branch.

DO GROUP :—Insert the longest stemmed rose just in front of the *Shin* branch. This should reach at least to the angle of separation between *Shin* and *Soe*.

TAI GROUP :—Select rosebud and cut about ⅓ of *Shin*. Insert leaning forward on Line 3. If this lacks leaves, insert leaves only so that *kenzan* is hidden.

TANI GROUP :—Add third rose on Line 2 at a different height from the other two. The three roses should form a triangle both in form and colour.

TOME GROUP :—Select a tall bunch of wild orchid leaves and bind them into shape about a seed-pod, do not cut. Insert in *kenzan* on Line 1. Now make two smaller bunches of the wild orchid leaves and cut at different heights—insert one bunch just in front of the *Do* rose and the other in front of the *Tani* rose.

NOTE :—The plum branch roots should be close together in the *kenzan* as though they were but one growing unit,—so also the roses. The addition of the wild orchid ties the two groups together as nature would.

Leave the strong line of the *Soe* branch exposed to suggest the trunk of a tree —do not add confusing small branches of the plum use the orchid leaves to soften the composition.

SHO-FU-RYU MORIMONO

Not a flower arrangement but closely following the rules that govern the positions of the different flowers in a floral composition; both fruit and vegetables are pressed into service to furnish a bit of beauty when flowers are not available.

SHO-FU-RYU MORIMONO

When flowers are scarce in the garden a handful of dried leaves and seed-pods will serve as a flower arrangement if carefully grouped on an interestingly shaped tray.

Chinese lilies with the bulb still attached make a pretty composition with small yellow chrysanthemums. An almost leafless branch of bitter-sweet is added for line. In Japan this combination of floral materials is to be found in very early Spring. Any flowers may be substituted. The idea suggested to the Japanese is that you have hurriedly gone into your garden and selected the best to be found and have set it forth for the delectation of your guest. These last-minute arrangements of fresh materials specially for a guest are much liked by the Japanese.

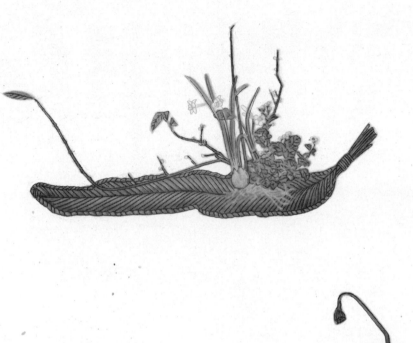

SHO-FU-RYU NAGEIRE

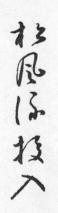

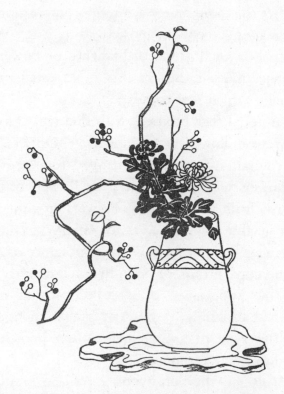

OF the three general divisions of Japanese flower arrangement, namely,—*Ike-no-bo*, *Moribana*, and *Nageire*,—*Nageire* is the style of arrangement most easily understood, and skill in its arrangement is most easily acquired, by Europeans. The name *Nageire* is applied to such diverse arrangements as that of a single white bud with its accompanying leaves, and that of an entire palm thrust into an immense container as decoration for a banquet hall.

Literally, *Nageire* means " thrown in," but for all its careless appearance, it is based on the same fundamental laws as the formal *Ike-no-bo*. Although an effect of naturalness is most necessary, the three groups of *Shin*, *Soe*, *Tai* retain the characteristics that they have in *Ike-no-bo* ; in fact the more nearly a *Nageire* composition approximates an *Ike-no-bo* arrangement the more pleasing it is. As in both *Ike-no-bo* and *Moribana*, each group of branches or flowers is triangular and complete in itself, but is also an essential part of the whole arrangement, which is triangular.

Any plant material may be used, with due regard to the rules governing all Japanese flower arrangements. Only such flowers as would grow naturally together are arranged together. Do not mix hot-house flowers with wild flowers, or flowers of the mountain-top with those from marsh land. Flowers growing in or near water are not as suitable for *Nageire* as for *Moribana* compositions. The finished arrangement should have the appearance of a growing unit, or a harmonious group of friendly, neighbourly growing plants. Avoid the appearance of a collection of isolated cut flowers. Any and all kinds of flowers, grasses or tree branches are suitable for this type of arrangement; often branches bearing fruit can be used to good advantage.

As with *Moribana*, the density of a *Nageire* arrangement is governed by the season of the year. Spring and Fall arrangements are fairly full ; those for Spring must express growth, buds and perfect flowers are suitable ; those for Fall must suggest the coming cold season, and for this the use of imperfect flowers and dry branches is appropriate. Winter arrangements are scant ; evergreen tree branches are most liked. Summer arrangements are full, a profusion of flowers is used ; often the coming Fall season is hinted at by the inclusion of a broken branch, or a dried seed-pod. In any season heavy branches are considered very suitable for *Nageire* ; their size and sturdiness suggest strength and continuity.

Cha-bana, or tea-flower, is one form of *Nageire*. It consists of a single blossom with its leaves. This is an extremely simple arrangement, but one which requires much skill.

It was developed, and is still used, by devotees of the tea ceremony. Perhaps a favourite flower for this is the white camellia, and a master of flower arrangement can suggest through the medium of one blossom the season of the year, or call to the mind of the beholder the picture of a peaceful spot in a great forest.

Very little bending is permissible, as naturalness is the keynote of a *Nageire* composition. The tips of the main branches should form a triangle, as should the colour mass of the flowers in the body of the arrangement. The ends of all branches should turn upwards as though growing; do not allow them to droop lifelessly.

Plants which naturally grow upright must be arranged so as to express this growing habit in the *Rittai*, or Standing Style.

271

Plants such as vines or bushes that naturally droop should be arranged in the Flowing Style—*Keishatai*.

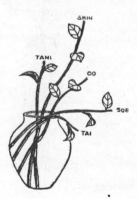

This is the usual method of holding flowers in the desired position in a *Nageire* arrangement; the ends of the stems rest firmly against the sides and bottom of the container. Note that all measurements given in the instructions are for the part of the branch which extends above the surface of the water; no allow-

272

ance is made for the part which extends below the surface of the water as that necessarily varies with the container.

Method of Holding Short Flowers or Branches in the Desired Position.

Insert one or more small twigs criss-cross in the container about an inch below the surface of the water and balance the stem of the flower against the twigs and the side of the container.

Sometimes a short stick or twig is inserted in the end of the flower ; this is suitable for tough plant material that can be split.

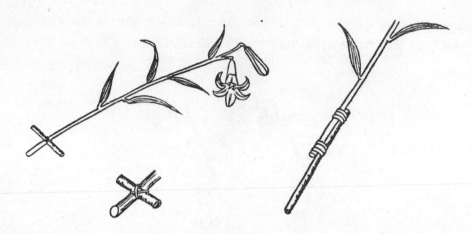

Method of fastening holder to plant material—such as soft-stemmed or brittle flowers.

Nageire compositions may be arranged in any vase or basket, but care must be taken that the completed arrangement does not look top-heavy. It is very essential that it have a balanced look. Large branches are best arranged in a very sturdy basket or bronze vase. Grasses and garden flowers totally insignificant in bronze containers make beautiful compositions if arranged in baskets. Narrow mouthed vases are seldom used, except for a single blossom and its leaves. The rule for *Nageire*, as for *Moribana*, is to leave half the mouth of the container free from flowers.

THIS style of arrangement is suitable for blossoms or plant material of stiff-growing habit. The blossoms of any fruit tree with a *Nejime* of flowers of contrasting colour make a pretty composition ; or irises, roses, carnations, etc., arranged alone.

SHIN GROUP

Cut flower bud or light-coloured flower equal to the height plus the widest width of the container. Or use branch with strong pretty tip and if possible bend to approximate the curve of the *Shin* branch of the *Ike-no-bo*. Insert upright, a little to the left of the centre of the container. Now complete this group by adding *Shin-ushiro*, *Shin-mae* and *Mikoshi*, as needed.

SOE GROUP

Use the same material as for the *Shin* group and cut main branch equal to ²/₃ the height of the *Shin*, or use flower bud if

275

using flowers only. Make this group triangular and complete by adding *Ushirozoe* and *Maezoe* if necessary. Insert so that *Soe* branch leaves the mouth of the container on Line 5.

DO GROUP

If the *Shin* and *Soe* groups are of tree branches make this a group of blossoms, or if flowers only are used select full-blown or dark-coloured flowers. There is no fixed height for this group and sometimes it is not necessary.

TANI GROUP

Select shortest plant material or full-blown or dark-coloured flower. Remember that this is the shortest part of the composition.

TAI GROUP

The *Tai* branch may be made of the same material as the *Shin* and *Soe* groups—or of the same as the *Do* and *Tani* groups. Cut the *Tai* branch itself $1/2$ the height of *Shin*. Insert so that branch leaves the mouth of the container between Lines 3 and 4. Add branches or flowers as needed behind the *Tai* branch, never in front. Keep in mind the shape of the *Nejime* of the *Ike-no-bo* arrangement and approximate that as nearly as possible.

STANDING STYLE ARRANGEMENT

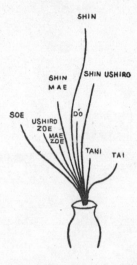

Hongatte or Right Hand Arrangement.

SHIN GROUP:—Cut main branch equal to the height plus the widest width of the container and insert so that branch leaves the mouth of the container about Line 6. Add branches as necessary in back and in front of this main branch.

SOE GROUP:—Cut main branch ⅔ the height of *Shin* and insert so as to leave container on Line 5. Add branches as necessary in front and in back of this branch.

DO and TANI GROUPS:—There are no fixed heights for these branches.

TAI GROUP:—Cut main branch ⅓ the height of *Shin* and insert so that branch leaves container between Lines 3 and 4. Add any necessary branches between this main branch and the *Shin* group.

277

STANDING STYLE ARRANGEMENT

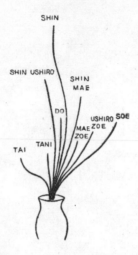

Gyakugatte or Left Hand Arrangement.

SHIN GROUP:—Cut main branch equal to the height plus the widest width at the container and insert so that branch leaves the mouth at Line 2. Add any necessary branches in back of and in front of this branch.

SOE GROUP:—Cut main branch ²/₃ the height of *Shin* and insert so as to leave container about on Line 3. Add any necessary branches in front of and in back of this main branch.

DO and TANI GROUPS:—There are no fixed heights for these branches.

TAI GROUP:—Cut main branch ¹/₃ the height of *Shin* and insert so that branch leaves container between Lines 4 and 5. Add any necessary branches between this branch and the *Shin* group.

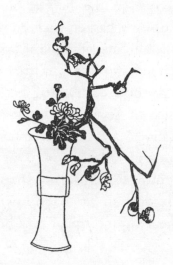

FOR this style of arrangement vines or plants of pliant material, or branches of an interesting shape, in combination with bright coloured blossoms, make a very pleasing combination. Be careful to observe the natural growing order of the plant material. Do not use a tree branch for the *Tai* if flowers are used for the *Shin* and *Soe*. Any Japanese arrangement must be a small part, or suggestion, of the garden outside the house.

Sometimes the *Shin* and *Soe* branches are made of flowerless tree branches, and the *Tai* and *Tani* of groups of blossoms. In this case the *Tai* group is called the *Nejime* by the Japanese. *Nejime* means "to hide or decorate the roots." When flowering branches are used for the *Shin* and *Soe* groups, the *Nejime* is often of flowers of a contrasting colour; sometimes a complementary colour is used.

SOE GROUP

Select a long drooping branch, or bend branch of pliant plant material and cut equal to the height of the container, plus the widest width. If using a basket, include the height to the top of the handle. This measurement is for the visible part of the branch; allowance must be made for the part that goes into the container. See page 273, for method of holding branch or flower in desired place. Insert branch or flower so that it leaves the mouth of the container about on Line 5. Add, if necessary, one or more branches or flowers, *Ushirozoe* and *Mikoshi*.

Make this group triangular in shape, and trim away superfluous flowers or leaves, so as to show the line of the stems. Make sure that the extreme tip of any branch points upwards as though growing.

SHIN GROUP

Use same material as for *Soe*. Select straight slender branch with pretty tip, or use flower bud. Cut equal to $1/2$ the height of the container. If plant material admits of it, gently bend this branch into the shape of the *Shin* branch of the *Ike-no-bo*. Insert in container upright on Line 6, just a little to the left of the centre of the container. The tip of the *Shin* branch of any Japanese flower arrangement must be over its base. Sometimes one branch or flower will suffice for the *Shin* group; if not add *Shin-ushiro, Shin-mae* and *Mikoshi*.

DO GROUP

Add branch or flower to thicken composition and tie the *Shin* and *Soe* groups together. There is no fixed height for this group, and sometimes it is not necessary.

TANI GROUP

This group also has no fixed height—it is the shortest and lowest part of the entire arrangement. For this and for the *Do* group full-blown or dark-coloured flowers are best.

TAI GROUP

This group, or more particularly the *Tai* branch itself, may be made of either the same material as the *Soe* and *Shin* groups, or of the same material as the *Do* and *Tani* groups. In either case cut the *Tai* branch ½ the height of the *Shin*. Tree or bush branches may be used for the *Shin* and *Soe* groups and for the *Tai* branch, and flowers for the *Do* and *Tani* groups to good advantage. Or *Tai* may be made of different material from that used in the *Shin* and *Soe* groups, but the same as that of the *Do* and *Tani* groups. Insert so that the *Tai* branch leaves the mouth of the container between Lines 3 and 4. Add branches or flowers behind the *Tai* branch, never in front, keeping in mind the shape of the *Ike-no-bo Nejime*.

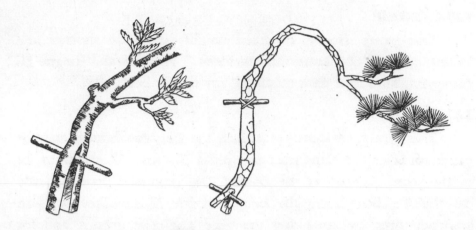

Method of holding a large branch in any desired position.

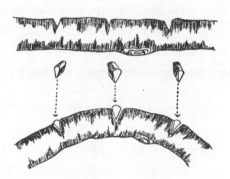

To hold a large tree branch or other tough plant material in the desired shape it is sometimes necessary to cut same halfway through and insert wedges of the same material.

The branches of many flowering trees, especially plum and cherry, must be bent sharply until the bark on the outside of the curve is broken or they will not retain the desired shape.

282

FLOWING STYLE NAGEIRE

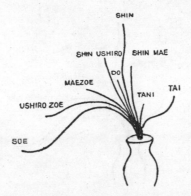

Hongatte or Right Hand Arrangement.

SOE GROUP:—Cut main branch equal to height plus width of widest part of container and insert so that branch leaves the mouth of the container about on Line 5.

SHIN GROUP:—Cut main branch equal to 1 $\frac{1}{2}$ the height of the container and insert so that branch leaves the mouth of the container about on Line 6.

DO and TANI GROUPS:—There are no fixed heights for these branches.

TAI GROUP:—Cut main branch $\frac{1}{2}$ the height of *Shin* and insert so that branch leaves container between Lines 3 and 4. Add any necessary branches between this branch and the *Shin* group.

FLOWING STYLE NAGEIRE

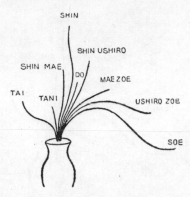

Gyakugatte or Left Hand Arrangement.

SOE GROUP:—Cut main branch equal to the height plus the widest width of the container and insert so that branch leaves the mouth of the container about on Line 3. Add necessary branches in front of and in back of the main branch.

SHIN GROUP:—Cut main branch equal to $1\frac{1}{2}$ the height of the container and insert so that branch leaves container about on Line 2. Add necessary branches in front of and behind this branch.

DO and TANI GROUPS:—There are no fixed heights for these branches.

TAI GROUP:—Cut main branch $\frac{1}{2}$ the height of *Shin* and insert so that branch leaves container between Lines 4 and 5. Add any necessary branches between this branch and the *Shin* group.

284

SHO-FU-RYU NAGEIRE

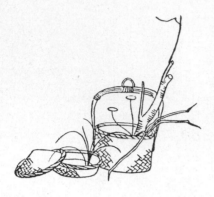

Gyakugatte or Left Hand Arrangement.

An interesting composition showing the intimate relationship between flowers and container, so much admired by the Japanese. The flowers used are extremely simple— mountain cherry, wild mustard and wild orchid—all mountain flowers. The arrangement is not only beautiful to look at but most pleasing in the associations it calls to mind. The delicate pink of the blossoms contrasted with the strength of the heavy branch and the red-brown of the Chinese lunch basket, conjure up happy days on a mountain side.

TO ARRANGE

SHIN GROUP :—This arrangement makes use of a heavy branch of the mountain cherry with its glossy reddish-brown bark. Trim off all small and confusing twigs, retaining only those that conform to the line of the main stem—sometimes it is necessary to bend these small branches into the desired shape. Cut branch equal to height (including handle) plus width of the basket. Insert between Lines 2 and 3 with extreme tip of branch over its base.

SHIN USHIRO :—Add slender branch with buds just behind the heavy branch and the least bit shorter.

SOE GROUP :—Now select a slender cherry branch with blossoms. Cut to ⅔ the height of *Shin* and gently bend into shape (the shape of the *Soe* branch of the *Ike-no-bo*). It should conform to the line of the main branch for four or five inches above the mouth of the basket.

USHIROZOE :—This branch also is unusual—a second cherry branch of interesting shape with a single perfect blossom at its tip attached to a branch with many blossoms—a little accentuation of the angle will throw this branch into position to be used as the *Tani* (or lowest) group of the arrangement. Insert on Line 3.

DO GROUP :—Two sprigs, of different lengths, of wild mustard and its leaves. Insert on Line 4 leaning slightly forward.

TAI GROUP :—In this arrangement it is outside the basket in the basket tray. A natural bunch of the wild orchid has been used, roots and all, after being washed to free them from earth. The lid of the basket is an integral part of the composition

NOTE :—A small porcelain bowl is placed in the basket to hold the flowers.

SHO-FU-RYU NAGEIRE

Hongatte Niju Nageire or Double Arrangement.

A charming arrangement of Easter lilies, carnation and fern—very Japanese in feeling. The containers play a very important part in the effect; note carefully the spacing of the two.

TO ARRANGE

The *Shin* and *Soe* groups are made of the Easter lilies while the carnation and fern form the *Tai* group. Use lily without cutting for longest branch and cut second lily about half the height of the first. Either the *Shin* or the *Soe* can be longest, your plant material will decide. If possible the longest lily should be two to three times the height of the container.

For *Tai* make a very simple *Shin-Soe-Tai* arrangement of the three carnations and some fern leaves.

SHO-FU-RYU NAGEIRE

Hongatte Shikisai or Right Hand Arrangement for Colour.

An arrangement for beauty of colour. Easter lilies and roses in a reddish-brown basket. This composition reflects the modern trend in Japanese flower arrangement, for while the shape and beauty of line are according to the old schools, the natural growing habits of the flowers have been ignored. A small bowl is placed in the basket, and flowers are inserted in that.

TO ARRANGE

SHIN GROUP :—Cut stalk of lily bud once and a half the height of the basket, measuring from base to top of handle. Gently bend into crescent shape. Insert in *kenzan* on Line 6, just to the left of the basket, in front of and not touching the handle. The tip of the bud should fall over the centre of the basket.

SOE GROUP :—Use half-open lilies—these may be allowed to droop as that is their natural growing habit. Cut ⅔ the length of *Shin* and insert on Line 5, leaning out over the edge of the basket to the left, and forward, but not touching the basket rim.

DO GROUP :—Use full-blown lily if possible. Insert in *kenzan* in front of *Shin* at a height just between the blossoms of *Shin* and *Soe*.

TANI GROUP :—Use three roses, cut to different lengths. Insert in *kenzan* in front of the *Do* lily, on Line 4.

TAI GROUP :—Select rosebud with naturally curved stem if possible; if not, gently bend stem into desired shape. No part of the branch should touch the basket. Insert in *kenzan* on Line 3 and be sure that the bud reaches upwards, it must not droop.

Now add three roses of different heights behind *Tai*, to bring this branch into harmony with the rest of the arrangement.

NOTE :—If roses of different colours are used, place darkest colours lowest. Buds are best used for higher branches regardless of colour, though a properly composed arrangement will have easily discernible triangular masses of colour as well as be triangular in its entire shape. The lilies and the roses should be inserted in the *kenzan* in separate groups as though two growing plants side by side.

SHO-FU-RYU NAGEIRE

Hongatte or Right Hand Arrangement.

A simple yet elegant arrangement of a moss-covered pine branch and white Easter lilies, in a beautifully wrought vase. This composition is æsthetically satisfying both in its design and symbolism. The dragon, to the Japanese, represents the quality of spiritual aspiration (never evil, as in Europe and America), and is here shown with the Jewel of Truth in its claw. The angular old pine branch covered with grey-green moss represents hoary old age and sturdiness, while the pure white lilies speak of beauty and the joy of youth. The arrangement pictured is from a photograph of a New Year decoration in the home of one of the Japanese Princes of the Blood, arranged by Mrs. Oshikawa.

TO ARRANGE

SHIN GROUP:—This arrangement makes use of a natural branch, therefore the lowest branch with its group of needles will be considered as the *Soe* group, and the upper group of needles as the *Shin*. Insert in the vase about on Line 5 and make it firm in its position by the use of a cross piece at the end of the branch. **(See page 282)**

In arranging pine be sure that the needles point upwards as though growing. Do not hesitate to cut off groups of needles which are not wanted in the composition.

DO GROUP:—Use full-blown lily—insert so that the line of the lily stem conforms to the line of the pine branch.

TANI GROUP:—Lily buds—insert conforming to the line of pine branch, but reaching directly forward over Line 4.

TAI GROUP:—Lily bud—follow line of pine branch as closely as possible, but lean buds forward on about Line 3.

NOTE:—No preservatives are necessary either for the lilies or pine. The pine will stay green for months; it should be sprayed with water occasionally to keep the needles fresh and free from dust. The "*Nejime*" or flowers can be renewed from time to time. Chrysanthemums or roses are equally suitable in place of the lilies.

292

SHO-FU-RYU NAGEIRE

Hongatte or Right Hand Arrangement.

This is a Summer arrangement of hydrangea, and, while the colour of the flowers is pleasing, the charm of the arrangement lies in beauty of line, and a sense of balance and proportion. The blue glazed pottery vase with its lovely soft colouring harmonises beautifully with the fresh green of the leaves, and the soft mauve of the flowers. The tall stand is a component part of the composition.

TO ARRANGE

SOE GROUP :—Select a well curved branch with fresh young blossoms at its tip. Cut so that when in vase it will extend about halfway to the floor. Carefully cut away most of the leaves so as to expose the main stem ; leave any dried branches, as this adds interest to the arrangement. Insert so that the branch leaves the vase at Line 5.

SHIN GROUP :—Select heavy-leaved branch without flowers, and cut twice the height of the vase. Insert at angle corresponding to the *Soe* branch, but upright at Line 6. Now add small tight bud in the rear of the *Shin* branch. If no bud is available use small blossom, or cut larger blossom down to suitable size. Any branch in the rear of *Shin* is considered as in the shade, and not fully developed.

DO GROUP :—Largest and prettiest blossom. Insert just in front of *Shin*, about in centre of vase.

TANI GROUP :—Add branch with pretty, full leaf-tip to right of *Do*.

TAI GROUP :—Leaf only—select a pretty group of leaves, and insert leaning forward at Line 4.

SHO-FU-RYU NAGEIRE

Hongatte or Right Hand Arrangement.

This is a simple arrangement but most attractive; a single morning-glory with a bud and a few leaves. A great deal depends on the background with such a fragile bloom. In the arrangement the soft tan-cream of the satiny wood panel and the cream of the simple woven basket form an ideal setting for the delicate beauty of the flower.

TO ARRANGE

SOE GROUP :—Select a long slender drooping bit of vine with a strong upward turning tip; without flowers is best. Cut long enough to extend about ⅔ the distance from the basket to the end of the panel. Insert so that vine leaves the basket mouth on Line 6. The basket should be hung so that the main flower will be about level with the eye.

USHIROZOE :—Now add another slender bit of vine just behind this first branch, reaching upward, not drooping. Insert so as to leave basket on Line 7, leaning well to the left.

SHIN GROUP :—Cut slender tendril about twice the height of the basket; if possible select branch with small bud; if not use only leaves. Insert upright on Line 8 with tip directly over its base.

MIKOSHI :—Add one long-stemmed strong leaf. Insert on Line 7 so that leaf stands erect between *Shin* and *Ushirozoe.*

DO GROUP :—Select one large open flower and insert in centre of the vine branches.

TANI GROUP :—Add small spray of small leaves as support to the flower, to the right of the flower but leaning forward over Line 4.

TAI GROUP :—Large strong leaf, long stem. Insert leaving basket on Line 4. In the arrangement illustrated leaves of variegated green have been used to give character to the composition.

NOTE :—Morning-glories will keep best if cut before sun-up and put in water immediately. It is well to provide yourself with a bottle of water in which sugar has been dissolved when gathering these blossoms; place them in it as soon as they are cut from the vine. When arranging, cut stems under water. A rusted pin stuck into the stem will aid in prolonging the life of this flower.

SHO-FU-RYU NAGEIRE

Hongatte or Right Hand Arrangement.

This arrangement consists of two entire banana palms and one yucca palm in a large sage-coloured vase standing on a slab of natural coloured wood. This is an arrangement suitable for a speaker's platform or hall decoration. It stands six to eight feet high.

TO ARRANGE

SHIN GROUP :—Use an entire banana palm cut about four times the height of the container. Fix this firmly upright a little to the left and front of the exact centre of the container.

SOE GROUP :—Use an entire yucca palm with blossom. Insert in container leaning a little to the front—have stem leave mouth of container about on Line 4, with blossom going to left of centre.

TAI GROUP :—Banana palm—cut stalk about ½ the height of the *Shin*—take leaves out of centre—use only two or three long sweeping leaves to give desired line.

SHO-FU-RYU NAGEIRE

Hongatte or Right Hand Arrangement.

An arrangement of three of the "seven flowers of Autumn." Yellow patrina, bluebell-flowers and themeda grass, arranged in a natural-coloured basket such as is used by flower gatherers, delicate and graceful.

TO ARRANGE

SHIN GROUP :—Use yellow patrina flower, cut equal to height plus width of the basket, insert upright in *kenzan* in bottom of water container, on Line 6.

SHIN USHIRO :—Insert slender bit of patrina, a little shorter han *Shin*, and bluebell-flower, to the rear of *Shin*.

SHIN MAE :—Insert piece of yellow patrina and bluebell-flower in front of *Shin*, but slightly to the left.

SOE GROUP :—Yellow patrina, ⅔ the height of *Shin*, insert in *kenzan* on Line 7, lean slightly forward to the left.

DO GROUP :—Use full-blown bluebell-flower, face flower forward.

TANI GROUP :—Use full-blown bluebell-flower, a little shorter than *Do;* lean well forward, about Line 4.

TAI GROUP :—Bell flower bud—⅛ the height of *Shin*, insert leaning over Line 3.

NOTE :—The yellow flowers form a triangle both in shape and colour, so also the bluebell-flowers. Now add grass sprays to soften and lighten the whole composition.

SHO-FU-RYU NAGEIRE

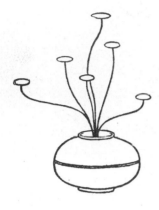

Hongatte or Right Hand Arrangement.

A composition showing a pair of vases, designed for use on a mantel-piece. This is a rather unusual arrangement in Japan, and beyond question greatly influenced by modern conditions. The vases, made in the shape of the Imperial chrysanthemum crest, are of Satsuma ware, decorated with chrysanthemums in colour; an interesting point of this composition is the use of the painted chrysanthemum in the pattern on the bowls as a part of the arrangement. The colour of the flowers reflects the colours on the bowls; shades of red, pink and mauve combined with the pink of the vases make a composition of rich beauty.

TO ARRANGE

Place large round *kenzan* in the bottom of the bowl and insert flower stems in it at desired angle—be sure to strip off all leaves below the mouth of the container. Instructions are given for the arrangement on the left—that on the right is the reverse in every respect.

SHIN GROUP :—Cut half-open yellow blossom the height plus the widest width of the flower bowl. Insert bolt upright on Line 5.

SHIN USHIRO :—Just behind this first blossom insert one a little shorter, to, the rear, on Line 8.

MIKOSHI :—Cut third chrysanthemum a little shorter than the second and insert on Line 7—incline it a little to the left.

SOE GROUP :—Cut half-open yellow chrysanthemum ⅔ the length of the *Shin* chrysanthemum and insert on Line 6, leaning well to the left.

DO GROUP :—Now add full-blown pink chrysanthemum at a suitable height, in front of *Shin*.

TANI GROUP :—Select full-blown perfect pink blossom as near the colour of that on the bowl as possible. Cut quite short. Insert on Line 4 and lean slightly forward. The painted chrysanthemum is considered as one of the *Tani* flowers of this arrangement.

TAI GROUP :—Now insert three dark red chrysanthemums at different heights—the one on Line 3 to be ⅛ the height of the *Shin* chrysanthemum, the other two to form a triangle both in height and colour.

SHO-FU-RYU NAGEIRE

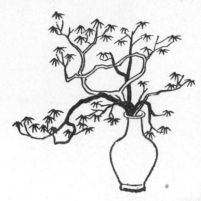

Hongatte or Right Hand Arrangement.

Two kinds of maple are used, a small fine-leaved green and a larger-leaved red maple. This arrangement is suitable for a speaker's platform or hall where a large decoration is needed to fill up space. In the picture a brown pottery vase is used standing on a dull red lacquered table.

TO ARRANGE

SOE GROUP :—Select a large fine-shaped branch of the green maple; it should be long enough to extend well beyond the table base. Cut off small branches so as to suggest a growing unit with leaves reaching upwards towards the sun. Trim so as to expose the line of the leaf branches. Insert in container at an angle leaving the container's mouth at Line 5.

SHIN GROUP :—Cut branch of red maple about twice the height of the container. Stand erect in middle of container.

TANI GROUP :—This is the shortest branch in the arrangement. Use red maple, taking care to select a full leaved branch. Insert leaning slightly forward leaving mouth of container at Line 4.

TAI GROUP :—Select long, slender, well-shaped branch of red maple cut long enough to balance the *Soe* branch. See that tip of branch turns upwards, never allow any tip to droop. Insert so that branch leaves mouth of container at Line 3. Now add a branch of green maple behind the *Tai* branch so as to avoid the appearance of two unrelated colour groups in the composition.

NOTE :—To keep maple, split ends of branches crosswise and insert peppercorns, or add salt to the water in which the branches are placed.

SHO-FU-RYU NAGEIRE

Hongatte or Right Hand Arrangement.

A Summer arrangement of great charm; simple, depending on grace of line and proportion for beauty, yet most satisfying. Bitter-sweet and mountain lilies arranged in a soft purplish-grey pottery dish, to be hung just at eye level.

TO ARRANGE

SOE GROUP :—Select a drooping branch of bitter-sweet with tip curving back strongly, and cut away all small and confusing branches so as to leave line of stem exposed. Cut length to hang about halfway to the floor. It may be necessary to bend this branch into the desired shape. Insert in *kenzan* in bowl so that branch leaves bowl over Line 5.

SHIN GROUP :—Cut about ⅛ length of *Soe*. Insert in *kenzan* on Line 7 to extend well forward at same angle as *Shin* so that tip is away from vase cords.

TANI GROUP :—Use full-blown mountain lily. Insert on Line 4; about ⅛ length of *Shin*.

TAI GROUP :—Select short branch of bitter-sweet with tip curving to left. Insert in *kenzan* on Line 3. Now cut lily bud about ½ the height of *Shin* and insert just behind the bitter-sweet and at the same angle, only face bud upward and toward body of arrangement.

NOTE :—Add half a dozen sprays of grass blades, or of long wild orchid, not many, just enough to soften the angles of the main branches.

SHO-FU-RYU NAGEIRE

Gyakugatte or Left Hand Arrangement.

A most attractive Autumn arrangement of a kind of bitter-sweet and large pink chrysanthemums in a blue vase of unusual colour and workmanship.

TO ARRANGE

SOE GROUP :—Select a well-shaped drooping branch of the bitter-sweet with a tip which curves up vigorously. Cut so that it will reach to just about the middle of the stand. Insert in vase on Line 3. It may be necessary to bind a cross-piece on the end of the branch to hold it firmly in place, and to keep it from turning. (See page 282)

SHIN GROUP :—Use heavy branch of the bitter-sweet, trim off all small and obstructing branches. Insert at an angle to follow the *Soe* branch where it leaves the vase, but so that the tip falls over the middle of the same. If such a heavy branch is not available, use the dry branch of any mountain bush, and add slender branch of the bitter-sweet, using one with many berries, in front of the *Shin*. Now add a slender branch to the right of *Soe* and between that and *Shin*. If arrangement is still too scant, add more than one.

DO GROUP :—Cut half-open chrysanthemum ½ the length of *Shin*. Insert in vase a little to the rear and to the left of *Shin*. Point tip forward slightly.

TANI GROUP :—Use full-blown chrysanthemum, shorter than first chrysanthemum. Insert between *Shin* and *Do*.

TAI GROUP :—Use chrysanthemum, cut to height of ⅓ of *Shin*. Insert in front of other chrysanthemum, extending forward on Line 5.

NOTE :—The three chrysanthemums form a triangle both in height and colour mass.

SHO-FU-RYU NAGEIRE

Hongatte or Right Hand Arrangement.

An elegant arrangement of orchid and Christmas roses in an old Chinese bronze vase. This is a modern arrangement, and much liked by the Japanese. The colour harmony is subtle; the daintiness and fragility of tne flowers add to the beauty of the composition and enhance the blue-green patina of the vase. The bronze vase used in the illustration is a thousand years' old incense-burner from China.

TO ARRANGE

SHIN and SOE GROUPS:—Both these branches are included in the one orchid spray. Place small *kenzan* in vase and insert orchid spray so that leaves point upwards—do not allow them to droop lifelessly. Lean spray at a slight angle on Line 5.

DO GROUP:—Insert tall Christmas rose about half as high as tip of *Shin*, to the right, leaning slightly to the rear. Now just in front of this insert full-blown Christmas rose.

TANI and TAI GROUPS:—Insert a third rose, quite short, in front of the arrangement, slightly to the right, with its leaves forming the *Tai* branch.

SHO-FU-RYU NAGEIRE

Hongatte or Right Hand Arrangement.

A classic arrangement appealing in its chaste simplicity and restraint. A single white camellia in an old bronze incense-burner. The white camellia is perhaps the favourite flower of the masters of Tea Ceremony. It is used in this composition to enhance the beauty of the old bronze.

TO ARRANGE

SHIN GROUP :—Select a straight branch with glossy leaves at the tip. Remove all leaves except two. Cut twice the height of the container and insert in *kenzan* upright and a little to the left of the centre of same.

SOE GROUP :—Select a full-blown flower with large glossy leaves. Cut away all but seven of the leaves, leave one large strong one on the left to serve as the *Soe* branch. Insert in front and a little to the left of *Shin*, leaning slightly forward.

TAI and TANI GROUPS :—Now look for a rugged strong branch with an up-springing slender branch. If this is not available bend one into the desired shape. Remove all leaves but one. This strong branch is needed to balance the whole composition and suggest natural growth.

SHO-FU-RYU NAGEIRE

Upper Arrangement.

A Winter composition of poinsettia and white roses, simple and easy to arrange. The dull red of the flat board under the white container adds greatly to the charm of the arrangement.

TO ARRANGE

SOE :—Use longest poinsettia—cut about twice the width of the container and insert in *kenzan* on Line 2 with the tip extending well over Line 5. Note that in the pictured arrangement this stem has been bent to approximate the *Soe* branch of an *Ike-no-bo* arrangement.

SHIN :—Cut second poinsettia ⅔ the height of *Soe* and insert in *kenzan* on Line 1, upright.

DO :—Use full-blown white rose—cut to height harmonious with *Shin* and *Soe*.

TAI :—White rosebud. Cut ⅓ the length of *Soe* and insert in *kenzan* on Line 2 leaning well forward with tip over Line 4.

Middle Arrangement.

Summer table ornament of two water lilies and five leaves in a brown hand-made pottery dish.

TO ARRANGE

Use two small *kenzan* and arrange as pictured.

Lower Arrangement.

Seven sprays of common garden pinks arranged in a fan-shaped dish. Suitable for a table decoration.

TO ARRANGE

Cut *Shin* about twice the width of the container and arrange according to simple Moribana, using *Shin, Shin-ushiro, Soe, Do, Tani, Tai, Tome.*

GLOSSARY

GLOSSARY

BAKUFU : Camp Government. The system of government established by Yoritomo at Kamakura under which all civil law was administered by the military with the Emperor in religious seclusion in Kyoto.

BUKKA : Flowers arranged in conformity with Buddhist art canons.

BUSHIDO : The unwritten teachings of self-mastery and magnanimity towards enemies as well as friends to which the military class of Japan was expected to conform.

CHA-BANA : Flowers arranged for the tea ceremony.

CHA-NO-YU : A formal and stylised method of making and serving tea developed and practised by the military class of Japan.

CHI : Earth.

CHICHI-HAHA : Father and mother.

DAI NIPPON KADO NO IEMOTO : Head (or Founder's) House of Flower Arrangement for Japan.

DO : Body or thickening.

FUTA-KABU : Divided root.

GYAKUGATTE : Left hand.

GYO-DO : Fish path. The term applied to one form of flower arrangement in which the stems of the flowers are separated so that it would be possible for fish to swim between them. Always arranged in a shallow flat container.

HANA : General term for all flowers, leaves, grasses and small bushes.

HANA-MI : Flower-viewing festivals.

HEIKA : General term for flowers arranged in vases.

HONGATTE : Right hand.

IEMOTO : Founder's house (or family).

IKE-BANA : Living flowers. General term applied to all flower arrangements.

IKE-NO-BO : Oldest school of flower arrangement in Japan.

JIN : Mankind.

KADEN : Secrets of flower arrangement.

KAMI : Gods or superiors.

KANSUI-IKE : Flowers arranged in square (or oval) flat, shallow containers so that the surface of the water is an important part of the composition.

KENZAN : Flower holders consisting of needles fastened upright in a block of lead.

KODOMO : Children.

KOJIKI : Ancient Japanese History, written in the early part of the seventh century.

KOMI : A short piece of plant material forced into the mouth of a vase to hold flowers upright in the holder.

KUBARI : Forked stick for holding flowers upright in a narrow-mouthed vase.

KOZO : Apprentice boy.

KUSA-BANA : Cut flowers.

KYOKU-SUI-NO-EN : Garden parties, or picnics, formerly held on the banks of running streams of water in celebration of the blossoming of different flowers, or when the maples were at their best.

MAE : In front of.

MAE NO NAKA-MIZU KANSUI-IKE : Flower arrangements in large, flat, shallow containers with a large group of flowers at the front and a smaller group at the rear of the container. The surface of the water between the two groups of flowers is an important part of the composition.

MIKOSHI : False perspective.

MORI-BANA : General term applied to all flower arrangements in shallow, flat containers, whether dishes, bowls or baskets.

MORI-MONO : General term for fruit, vegetables, flowers (without water) or stones arranged according to the rules for flower arrangement.

NAGEIRE : General term for all arrangements in tall vases or baskets.

NAKA-MIZU : Flower arrangements in medium-sized, flat, round containers with two groups of flowers showing the surface of the water between them.

NEJIME : Term used by the Ike-no-bo school of arrangement to designate the shortest group of the arrangement when it is made of different plant material from the other two groups.

NIHON SHOKI : Ancient Japanese History, written about the end of the seventh century.

320

OKU :   In the rear.

OKU NO NAKA-MIZU KANSUI-IKE :   Same as Mae no Naka-mizu Kansui-ike but with the larger group of the arrangement in the rear of the container and the smaller group to the front.

O-MIKOSHI :   Portable shrine carried by villagers through the streets in celebration of shrine festivals.

OSHI-ITA :   Fore-runner of the tokonoma.

RIKKA :   Standing flowers.

SAKAKI :   A kind of evergreen used for floral offerings at all Shinto ceremonies.

SAKE :   The national wine of Japan, made from rice.

SAMURAI :   Knight or military man.   Anciently recruited from the farmers on the land ; during the twelfth century this calling became hereditary.   Only the eldest son of a family succeeded to the title.

SASHI-BANA :   Flowers arranged in a vase.

SHIKISAI :   Colour harmony.

SHIN :   The term applied to the main central branch of any Japanese flower arrangement.

SHIN-NO-HANA :   Ancient form of the Ike-no-bo school of flower arrangement.

SHINKA :   Flowers arranged according to Shinto art canons.

SHINTO :   The indigenous religion of Japan.

SHOGETSU-DO :   One of the many modern schools of flower arrangement.

SHO-FU-RYU :   The school of flower arrangement set forth in this book.

SOE :   The term applied to the intermediate branch (or group of branches) of the flower arrangements illustrated in this book.

SUMI-YE :   Black and white drawings done in India ink.

TAI :   The term applied to the third and lowest branch (or group of branches) in the arrangements illustrated in this book.

TANI :   Valley.

TATE-BANA :   Standing flowers.

TATAMI :   Straw mats used as flooring in Japanese homes.

TENNO :   Emperor.

TOKONOMA :   An ornamental recess in a Japanese room.

TEN :   Heaven.

TOME : Stopper, or false horizon line.

UJI-GAMI : Clan heads (or leaders) in ancient Japan.

UKIYO-YE : Genre paintings developed about the middle of the seven-teenth century, known outside of Japan as " Japanese prints."

USHIRO : Behind.

USUBATA : Conventional vase for Ike-no-bo arrangements the distinguishing feature of which is a plate-like top section.

ZEN : A contemplative sect of Buddhism, especially favoured by the military class of Japan.

NOTE :—The small designs scattered throughout the pages of this book are Japanese " mon " or family crests. The coloured illustrations are reproductions of photographs of arrangements made by the authors ; while the line drawings are sketches of standard arrangements.